TRAVEL SURROGATES

TRAVEL AGENCY AND TOUR OPERATION MANAGEMENT

ANAGHA SATHEESAN TM

Copyright © Anagha Satheesan Tm
All Rights Reserved.

DEDICATED TO ALL THE BABY FLOWERS THAT FALL OFF BEFORE BLOOMING.

ANAGHA SATHEESAN TM

Contents

PREFACE

People can travel almost everywhere in the world because of modern transportation and communication technologies, and the rapidly growing hospitality sector provides accommodations for them once they arrive. The business of travel agencies has witnessed buoyant growth in recent years. This upbeat sector provides enormous income and employment opportunities and offers complete travel solutions to new-age travellers. In the beginning, the travel agency business was in a state of experimentation and community help. Gradually, the business grew up on such a scale that competitive travel companies around the world forged into the sophisticated business.

As a travel professional or planning to be a travel professional, you need to know a lot more than the travel professional of the past. Nowadays, the choice available to today's travellers is more varied than ever before. There is an increasing demand for travel industry professionals and the need for specialized training for travel professionals. This book brings together the best practices for growth, development, travel business strategies, and practices for the organizations to obtain a competitive management model at a global level within the tourism and hospitality industries.

ANAGHA SATHEESAN TM

Acknowledgements

"Be thankful for what you have" you'll end up having more. If you concentrate on what you don't have, you will never, ever have enough. The roots of all goodness lie in the soil of appreciation for goodness."

Nothing is more important than expressing gratitude to all who have stood tirelessly on my side to complete this work.

Dear God, Thank you so much for the amazing journey you have taken me on.

Everything I am is because of you people. Thank you for all that you have done for me Achan N Amma.

"A good teacher is like a candle – it consumes itself to light the way for others." thank you to all teachers who light me up even brighter and sharper.

Thank you Babi ettan n Nanooz for motivating me even when I wanted to give up........

Thank you Prasoon ettan for fueling my passion and for the inspiration you created in my life.

Thank you to all my students, friends, and relatives who have one or another way paved my way.

ANAGHA SATHEESAN TM

I

THE NOTION OF INTERMEDIARIES

*SATISFACTION FROM "I'M PROVING" IS SHORT.
HAPPINESS FROM IMPROVING IS PERMANENT"
~TAU*

When did tourism really begin? We can't pinpoint it and, for obvious reasons, we can only really guess about tourism in ancient times. There are no selfies or travel brochures to look back on, but we know that people DID travel in ancient times. Historians have found records that provide an insight into the reasons that people travelled, and how this evolved into tourism.

The phrase "travel trade" was first used in the early nineteenth century, but this should not hide the reality that what we now call "travel commerce" occurred far earlier in history. Travel intermediaries have existed throughout history to assist businessmen travelling for trade and those travelling for religious reasons.

TRAVEL INTERMEDIARIES

Travel intermediation is a business activity that consists of mediating the sale and organization of tourism services. This activity includes organizing and marketing packaged trips, one-day tours, selling tickets, booking seats on all means of transportation, booking or contracting tourist accommodation, and booking services and activities offered by tourism companies.

A travel intermediary is a distribution agent that participates in the sale and/or brokerage of travel and tourism-related products and services. Travel intermediaries act as middlemen between suppliers and consumers, buying and reselling products and services related to tourism. For instance, a B2B tour operator can sell one-day tours to a travel agent, who then sells them to consumers.

TOURISM INTERMEDIARY

Tourism intermediaries are distribution agents that participate in a tourism-product sales process from its creation until the time it is consumed by final clients. Most intermediaries are wholesalers, tour operators, bed banks, booking centres, DMCs and OTAs (online travel agencies).In the tourism industry, travel agents, tour operators etc. are considered the intermediaries.The role of the travel suppliers is to provide travel and transport-related services to consumers. Because of the intangibility of the tourism product, they rely on the distribution of information. Travel intermediaries may be divided into wholesalers and retailers.

Any person who assists in the distribution of travel products to travellers is a travel intermediary. Online intermediaries are also growing. Job profile: Travel agency intermediaries may sell airline tickets, book accommodation, tours and attractions, do ticketing and process payments. A tour operator typically combines tour and travel components to create a package holiday. They advertise and produce brochures to promote their products and holidays.

DISTRIBUTION CHANNELS IN TOURISM

A distribution channel is considered a vehicle utilised to make a product or service available to the consumer. A tourism distribution channel is a network of intermediaries that facilitates the sales and delivery of products and services specifically related to tourism from suppliers to consumers. The concept of distribution channels is not limited to the distribution of physical goods. Tourism services require simultaneous production and consumption, meaning the product is not normally 'moved' to the consumer.

A tourism distribution channel may be defined as a total system of linkages between actual and potential tourists and suppliers. Distribution in tourism is the transfer of tours and related facilities from suppliers to tourists through a system. A distribution channel is used for indirect selling and it involves all those who are providing the product from the supplier to the tourist.

FUNCTIONS OF DISTRIBUTION CHANNELS IN TOURISM

A good distribution channel eases the effort of the manufacturer to reach the customer and it also ensures a smooth flow of products and services in the chain. The entire process of deciding the channel, managing the intermediaries, ensuring the inventories and making it available at the point of sale needs to be taken care of. There are two aspects of distribution

i. Handle enquiries and sales on behalf of the supplier or principal
ii. Physical delivery of products to channel and ultimately to the customers.

Tourism products are service-focused, and therefore the distinctive nature of the tourism business, and the decisions of distribution channels are complex.

The tourism industry is made up of many distinct enterprises. Tourism service providers have a dual function to play they are both suppliers and retailers. A hotel room can be sold to a walk-in customer or through an internet portal or mobile app.

The distribution channels serve as key information sources for travellers seeking information about the destination's attractions and activities. Some of these channels sell a variety of products or services, while others specialise in a single service. The distribution channel members' responsibility is to have a general awareness of the places, numerous activities that may be done, and the destination's unique qualities.

LEVELS OF DISTRIBUTION

Distribution channels are of different types and an organisation may adopt any one type or combination of all the types. All this depends on the type of service being provided by an organisation. Various levels of distribution channels include.

1. **Single-level Channel:** Here the service is directly distributed to the consumers. For example, Airlines directly book the tickets for the customers or hotels book rooms for guests.

2. **One Level Channel:** It implies a single level where only one type or category of the middleman is used. The service industry is predominantly using this kind, For example, airlines use travel agents for booking seats for air travel. There is only one intermediary between the service supplier and the service user.

3. **Two-Level Channel:** In this case, the distribution of services is through two intermediaries. For example, in the airlines, GSA and, travel agents form two levels of distribution channel.

4. **Multi-Level Channels:** Many times, more than two categories of intermediaries are simultaneously used in the service industry and this is particularly the case in the tourism and travel industry. For example, lodging or attractions or carriers may sell their services to incentive travel planners, in turn, these incentive travel planners sell the services to convention meeting planners or corporate travel managers. Similarly, wholesale tour planner sells their services to travel agents and tour operators.

II

AN ARCHIVES TO TRAVEL AGENCY

"Do not follow where the path may lead. Go instead where there is no path and leave a trail"

– Ralph Waldo Emerson

A Travel agency is a "One-stop" shop. The minute a traveller thinks of extensive travel, he or she thinks of a travel agency. A travel agent has to, therefore, add value to the company and the traveller. A Travel Manager person who specialises in packaging the required services.

"A travel agency is a private retailer or public service that offers several types of travel packages for each destination on behalf of hotel or travel suppliers. Outdoor recreation activities, airlines, car rentals, cruise lines, hotels, railways, travel insurance, package tours, insurance, guide books, VIP airport lounge access, arranging logistics for luggage and medical items delivery for travellers on request, public transportation schedules, car rentals, and bureau de change services are all services that travel agencies can provide. Airlines that do not have operations in a specific location can use travel companies as broad sales agents."

A travel agency's main function is to act as an agent, selling travel products and services on behalf of a supplier. Travel agencies are frequently compensated by providers with commissions and other bonuses and incentives, or they may charge a fee to end-users. Travel agencies often receive a greater commission from hotel owners and tour operators, whereas airlines receive a lower commission.

THE PIONEERS

In the beginning, the travel agency business was in a state of experimentation and community help. Gradually, the business grew up on such a scale that competitive travel companies around the world forged into the sophisticated business. The nature of the business was a sort of intermediary role to cater holiday-related services to those who were away from home. Travel agencies made all possible efforts to ensure the service quality for enhancing the level of satisfaction.

In 1670, the Grand Tour concept was developed especially for educational purposes. Another major development took place in the year 1730. Health experts suggested that seawater is found to be useful to cure many diseases. The result was that many resorts around the English Coast were established to attract visitors seeking to cure themselves with seawater. In 1815, steamboat services were introduced from London to Gravesend. One effect of this development was the construction in all major resorts of a pier to accommodate the vessels on their arrival. In 1820, European cultural centres were opened to British travellers. The rail link was introduced between Liverpool and Manchester in 1830. In 1838, the Peninsular and Oriental (P&O) Steam Company introduced steamship services to India and the Far East

· *Cox & Kings*

Cox & Kings Ltd., set up in 1758, is one of the longest-established travel companies. Headquartered in India and the UK. They are providing travel logistics to British Army stationed at various locations in the world. It claims to be the oldest travel agency in the world. The Company became the most reliable military agent of the British Government. In the subsequent period, business got expanded to banking, shipping, and tour operations business. Being a 250-year-old company serving leisure and business travellers, it maintains business and operational networks across the world. Cox & Kings Ltd. has operations spread across 22 countries and 4 continents. It was declared bankrupt in 2020 and is undergoing bankruptcy proceedings under Indian Insolvency and Bankruptcy Code.

· *Abreu Agency*

Bernardo Abreu founded the Abreu Agency in Porto in 1840, making it the world's first agency to open its services to the general public. It is the largest travel organization in Portugal. Thus, the oldest travel agency in the world was created from the close ties Portugal and Brazil still enjoy. After World War II, as the growth of commercial aviation shortened the distances between continents and international tourism expanded, Abreu developed into its current organization. Five generations later, the company is still owned by the same family and their direct descendants.

· *The Thomas Cook Group*

In 1841 a fortunate day comes in the history of the travel trade when Thomas Cook, as secretary and a Baptist preacher who believed that alcohol was to blame for social problems, of the South Midland Temperance Association, organized a trip by train for 570 members for his association to the distance of 22 miles. He bought railway tickets in bulk to sell them to people.

The experiment was successful and everybody was exultant. Mr Cook had done his job on a no-profit basis. But incidentally, it gave him a new idea and turned it into a tour business. The company's first excursion was a one-day rail trip, from Leicester to Loughborough and back; the price of one shilling included a meal. This has been described as the world's first package tour

Four years later in 1845, he set up a 'World's First Travel Agency 'to organize excursions. Due to this innovative approach, Mr Thomas Cook is known as the Father of the Travel Agency Business. He coordinated railway and steamship excursions throughout England, Scotland and Europe.

However, the railways only gave him a 5% commission which was not enough to meet his overheads, so he decided to diversify this business into tour operation. In 1855 Mr Cook started operating package tours. He conducted the world's first international tour from England to Paris. This was an inclusive tour and, in this way, he developed the concept of an inclusive tour. From its humble beginnings, Thomas Cook steadily grew, adding more destinations and holidays and it becomes the second-largest European travel group. Later he formed Thomas Cook & Son, which later became The Thomas Cook Group. It filed for bankruptcy and underwent liquidation in 2019.

THEORY OF TRAVEL AGENCY

Definition of Travel Agency:

A Travel Agency may be an individual, a business firm, or a company which acts as an intermediary in the sales and promotion of different travel-related services, such as accommodation, airlines, railways, road transports cruise, etc and earn commission received on selling service services to its clients.

A Travel agency can also be referred to as a retail travel agency since it sells the various services offered by the travel supplier directly to its customers.

Travel agent:

An individual who arranges travel for individuals or groups. Travel agents may be generalists or specialists, for their service in return they get a fixed percentage commission. They typically coordinate travel for their customers at the same or lower cost than if the customer booked the travel on his/her own.

TYPES

Travel agencies are categorized into two types-: Retail Travel Agency and Wholesale Travel Agency

RETAIL TRAVEL AGENCY

According to SARC (1967), " retail travel agency business consists of the activities involved in selling tourism products/services directly to the tourists and performs normal functions such as issuing air tickets, making accommodation and transportation reservation, providing specialized services, and accepting and making payments".

A retail travel agency operates similarly to any other store, selling tourist products directly to visitors on behalf of the supplier and earning a commission. Its primary source of revenue is commission. A two-way selling approach based on commission and mark-up price is also used. A marked-up price refers to the marking-up of the cost of the tour and selling it at a higher price. The difference between retail price and wholesale cost is known as mark-up price.

WHOLESALE TRAVEL AGENCY

These agencies are specialized in organizing package tours, which are marketed to the customers/tourists through the network of a retail travel agency or directly to the prospective clients if the wholesale travel agency has a retail division. A wholesale travel agency purchases tourists' product components in bulk and designs tour packages.

A wholesale travel agency may purchase travel components in bulk from a provider and resell them to other travel businesses. Wholesale travel agencies put together vacation packages that retail travel agencies sell to customers. A typical package tour comprises air tickets, lodging, and sometimes extra services such as entertainment, sightseeing, and sports activities, among others. The majority of these cruises include the services of escorts, however, a handful is sold to customers who want to go solo.

There are many ways in which travel agencies can be further classified. Travel agencies are generally classified as follows:

FULL-SERVICE TRAVEL AGENCY

A full-service agency organizes and handles all types of tours for leisure, free individual travellers (FITs), group individual travellers (GITs), corporate travellers, etc inbound, outbound, and domestic destination. Individual departments work on the different functions of a travel agency, for example, the leisure department, inbound department, outbound department, trade fairs, accounts, etc.

COMMERCIAL TRAVEL AGENCY

Commercial agencies are specialized in meeting the requirements of corporate travellers. Such agencies are mainly located in the business centre and cater only to business travellers. Walk-in or individual travellers are not served by these agencies. The airline, hotel, car/coach, documentation. etc, are all looked after by the trained staff.

IMPLANT AGENCY

It is a branch office of a full-fledged travel agency/tour operator functioning on the premises of a corporate office. It handles all travel arrangements of the corporate office.

SPECIAL INTEREST TRAVEL AGENCY

Specialize in creating tour programs for special interest groups, such as adventure, wildlife, religions etc.

E-TRAVEL AGENTS OR ONLINE TRAVEL AGENTS (OTA)

Also known as virtual/ online travel agents (VTA's) or e-retailers, they are the new generation of travel agents such as MakeMyTrip.com, Yatra.com, ezego1.com, Travelgure.com, and lastminute.com. These web portals allow consumers to access information and make online bookings.

FUNCTIONS

The functions performed by a travel agency depend upon the scope of activities size and location. The following are the major functions performed by the travel agency

1. Provision of Travel Information

Information is the first and foremost function of a travel agency. This is a very specialized job and the person behind the counter should be a specialist. A good travel agent is something of a personal counsellor who knows all the details about the travel and also the needs and interests of the intending traveller.

2. Liaison with Providers of Services

In the travel trade, there are a lot of intermediaries are involved, before any form of travel can be sold over the counter, contracts have to be entered into with the principal providers of various services. These include transportation companies, hotel proprietors, surface transport like motorcars or coaches for transfers to and from hotels for sightseeing, etc.

3. Identification of profile of target market

The travel agency has to select a particular market segment it wants to cater to because possibly one cannot serve all kinds of clients effectively. Once a particular market segment or more than one segment is selected, he has to prepare their profile i.e. what age, sex, income, education, and social groups they belong to because ultimately there, preference for destination, transport and accommodation and purchasing power depends upon these factors.

4. Preparation of tour Itineraries

A tourist itinerary is a composition of a series of operations that are a result of the study of the market. A tourist journey is characterised by an itinerary using various means of transport to link one locality with another. The preparation of different types of itineraries is another important function of a travel agency. The development and implementation of itineraries necessitate flawless technological and administrative organisation, as well as awareness of public holiday desires.

5. Ticketing

Another significant duty of a travel agency is to sell tickets to clients for various modes of transportation such as air, rail, and sea. Due to frequent changes in international and domestic airline schedules, as well as the arrival of new flights, the job of the travel agent has been more difficult in recent years.A computerised reservation system (CRS) has rather revolutionised the reservation system both for air and rail seats and also a room in a hotel.

6. Documentation and foreign exchange procedures

If the travel includes an international journey, the travel agent is responsible to make necessary arrangements for travel documents, which are needed to enter a foreign country like passport, visa, health documents etc... No trade can take place without the presence of forex, the conversion of one country's currency into another.Approved travel agency authorized by Govt. body provides currency exchange services to tourists.

7. Reservation and Booking

It is a very important function of all types of travel agencies. A travel agency consistently makes linkage with the accommodation sector, transport sector and other entertainment organizations to reserve rooms, and seats in the cultural programs and transportation.

8. Travel Insurance

It is a very important function of all types of travel agencies. A travel agency consistently makes linkage with the accommodation sector, transport sector and other entertainment organizations to reserve rooms, and seats in the cultural programs and transportation.

9. Preparation, costing and marketing of tour package

Travel agencies prepare and market tour packages and sell them to tourists. The coasting and pricing of tour packages depend to a large extent on the ability of travel agents to how effectively he can negotiate with the principal suppliers.

10. Meeting and Incentive Planning

The business events sector is one of the highest-yielding inbound tourism segments. Meeting and incentive planners organise and manage all aspects of meetings and events including conventions, conferences, incentives, seminars, workshops, symposiums, exhibitions and special events. Meeting and incentive planners use a wide variety of venues, tour operators, accommodation, team building companies and restaurants.

III

KEY WORK ROOMS

"If we were meant to stay in one place, we'd have roots instead of feet"

– Rachel Wolchin

ORGANISATIONAL STRUCTURE OF TRAVEL AGENCY

The organization of a travel/ tour company largely depends on the size and type of the business handled by it. Generally, in a small and medium-scale travel agency/ tour operator, one will find a simple organisational structure being limited in terms of operation, size, division of labour and so forth. Whereas in large-scale travel companies the organisational structure is more formal.

A sound organizational structure of a travel company brings the following benefits to the travel business:

· Develop sound and up-to-date management practices, systems and strategies.

· Develop effective leadership.

· Growth and diversification.

· Optimum use of 'human asset'.

· Stimulates creativity.

· Effective coordination between various departments

The organisational structure of a Travel agency can divide into two parts:

(1) Organization structure of large Scale travel agency /standard Travel agency.

(2) Organization structure of Small scale Travel agency

ORGANISATION STRUCTURE OF LARGE /STANDARD TRAVEL AGENCY:

Large scale travel agency has its qualified staff and skills dominated in major cities of the world. Both types of travel agencies produce the managers of each department accordingly. Each to deliver the enteric product and service package to the tourist.

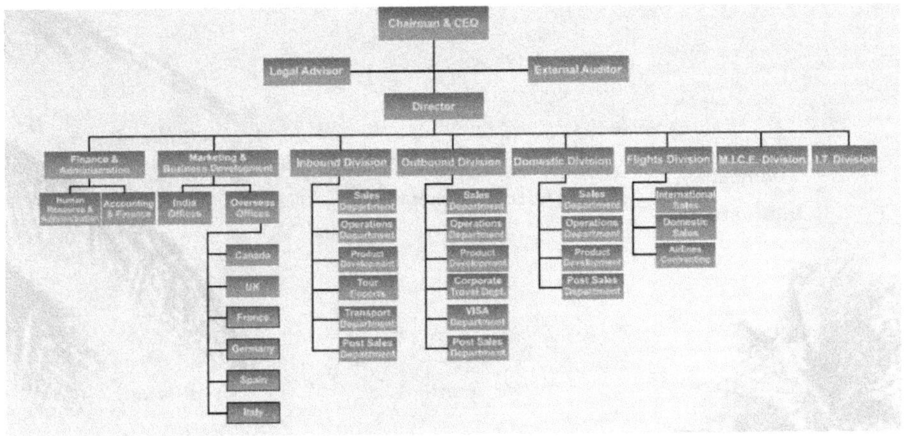

ORGANISATIONAL CHART OF TRAVEL AGENCY

The chart depicts the visible superstructure of departments and the important reporting and functional relationships in the organization of a travel company. The structure consists of a managerial hierarchy from top-level to junior-level managers and assistants. Normally, a large-scale travel company has two parts Head Office and several branches within the country and abroad. It is also common that the headquarters/registered offices would have several divisions such as research and planning, travel and tour division etc. and so forth. However, in the branches, one will find a few departments according to the requirements of specialized particular areas. Obviously, in designing an organisational structure a travel company is free to use any means of departmentation that are appropriate to its business operation, type of customer- traveller corporation, its services and specific functions and activities to achieve a mission or goals and the core values etc.

ORGANISATION STRUCTURE OF SMALL-SCALE AGENCY:

A small-level travel agency can have a tie-up with another small size of tourism supplier.

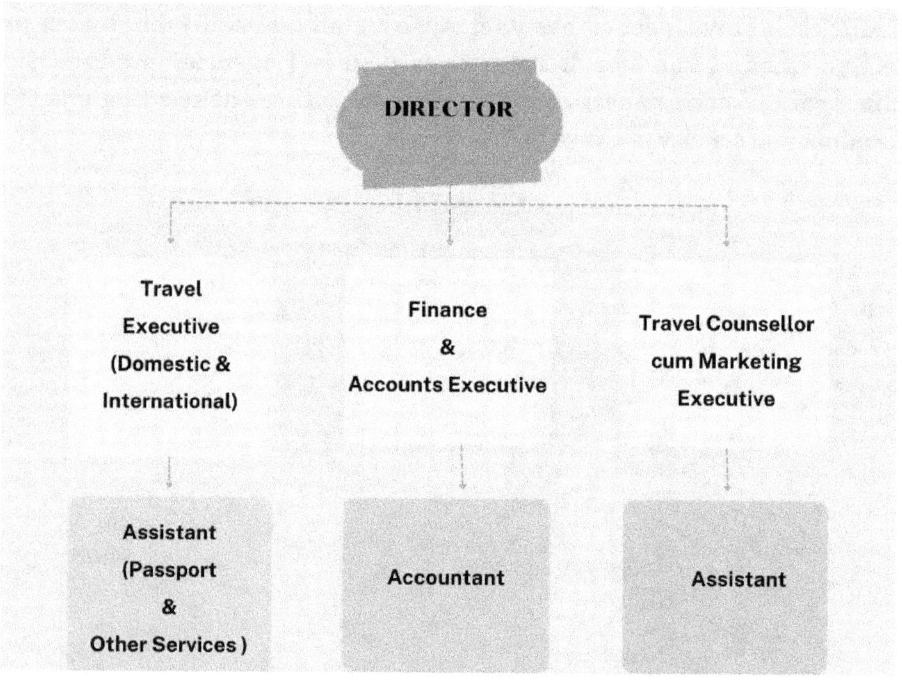

ORGANISATION STRUCTURE OF SMALL TRAVEL AGENCY

SETTING UP OF TRAVEL AGENCY

There are no legal criteria for starting a travel agency. However, in certain nations, the government regulates agencies through licencing. The sale of most principals' services is licenced through the use of an agency contract or agreement. A travel agency will not receive any commission from selling the service on behalf of the principal if there is no such contract or agreement. A travel agent's only source of income is the commission they earn from the principal after selling their services.

For setting up a travel agency one has to take into account the following aspects:

- Infrastructural and financial requirements,
- Approvals from concerned bodies,
- Recognitions from principal suppliers,
- Incentive and benefits

1. Infrastructural and Financial Requirements

For starting a new business in this area the capital requirements are not very high. The requirements in this regard require investment for the following:

- Buying or hiring of office space,
- Office furniture and furnishings,
- Communication equipment (like fax, telephone, Xerox, computers, etc.),
- Salaries for the staff, and
- Office materials (like files, labels, promotional brochures, letterheads, etc.)
- These capital requirements are not too high and because of this, we find several persons entering this business. (For raising funds to meet capital requirements)

2. Approvals by Concerned Bodies

A travel agency requires certain approvals for the business and in this regard, an approval from the International Air Transport Association (IATA) which is the World Organisation of Scheduled Airlines, is very useful. IATA has worked out international fares and rates and uniform transportation documents to facilitate the carriage of passengers and cargo worldwide. An IATA-approved Passenger is an Agent who is capable of receiving commissions on International Air Travel documents. This commission is paid only to approved Agents.

To apply for IATA approval, an application has to be submitted, by filling the requisite forms, and sent to the Secretary, Agency Investigation, of IATA. In this regard the following aspects are checked:

- Ability to generate and procure air passenger transportation,
- Professional standing,
- Financial status,
- Business premises, and
- Staff ability and experience

A final inspection is held and the approval is given by IATA. IATA Agents get a 9% commission on international air tickets and 6% on domestic airline tickets.

3. Recognition and Licences

A must seek recognition from the Department of Tourism Government of India and also take licences from the principal suppliers like the airlines and Reserve Bank of India along with recognition from the hotels are necessary for earning commissions on the business carried out.

Department of Tourism

The Department of Tourism, Government of India has set certain rules for a travel agency and it gives a one-time approval. This recognition is given to those agencies only that have been in operation for at least one year.

Reserve Bank of India Licence

To receive and deposit foreign exchange earned, with a Bank the agency should have a Restricted Money Changer's Licence and proper returns must be filed with the Reserve Bank of India every fortnight.

According to regulations, Indian Airlines has dollar fares for foreign tourists and there are incentives given by the Government for foreign exchange earnings, so this licence and record are very important to register foreign exchange earnings.

Hotel Recognition

Once a travel agency is recognised by the Department of Tourism, most hotels (whether they are 5 stars, 4starsr, 3-Star or Budget) and leading hotel chains will automatically give commission on business handled by a travel agency. The department of Tourism's recognition gives creditability to the travel agency. It gives a standing in the industry and the hotels feel reassured that their bills will be paid. Depending upon the volume of business, hotels may give 10% commission and credit and sometimes even an overriding commission.

At times special rates are negotiated to keep in view the volume of business. A good travel manager must know the art of negotiating special rates to maximise revenue.

Travel agencies should also establish linkages with tour operators, tourist transport operators, tourist cargo operators, etc, along with getting recognised by the railways and state tourism development corporations.

4. Incentives and Benefits

An incentive or benefit is a payment or concession to stimulate greater output or investment.

The Government of India gives certain incentives and benefits to the tourism industry and a person intending to set up a travel agency to promote the industry. For example:

- Financial benefits are available under Section 80HHD in The Income-Tax Act, 1995 to the travel agents and hoteliers. Under this 50% of earning profits in foreign exchange are free of income tax and the other 50% are also tax-free if they are ploughed into the development of tourism.

- The Department of Tourism gives prizes to various categories of travel agencies for foreign exchange earnings. This is an honour that acts as an incentive to boost foreign exchange earnings by the travel agency.
- The Tourism Finance Corporation gives loans to persons for setting up travel agencies. Department of Tourism, Government of India provides brochures, tourism-related data, etc. to travel agencies for promotional purposes.
- The Department of Tourism, Government of India also assists the travel agencies with participation in tourism fairs, travel marts, and official promotional delegations. Generally, such is provided through the Travel Agents Association of India and it is advisable should become members of TAAI (TRAVEL AGENTS ASSOCIATION OF INDIA)

BILLING AND SETTLEMENT PLAN – BSP

BSP or Billing and Settlement Plan is an IATA electronic billing system to run and simplify the interchange of data and funds between travel agencies and airlines. BSP is a payment mediator between airlines and travel agents,BSP collects payments from agents and distributes them across airlines.

BSP acts as a single point of remittance and settlement of money. Without it, each travel agent would have to connect individually with every single airline. BSPs are organized oBSPsocal basis, usually one per country. However, there is some BBSPswhich cover more than one country.

BSP is truly a worldwide system its operations in some 180 countries and territories. The system currently serves more than 370 participating airlines with an on-time settlement rate of 99.999%. In 2017, IATA's BSP processed $236.3 billion.

Benefits of a BSP

Simplification

- Agents issue one sales report and remit one amount to a central point

- Airlines receive one settlement covering all agents
- Simplifies and reduces work through the use of electronic ticketing on behalf of all BSP Airlines
- Agents' sales are reported electronically

Savings

- Limited resources are required for billing and collection
- Electronic distribution of billing reports and generation of debit/credit memos (ADMs/ACMs) via BSP link

Enhanced Control

- Increased financial control because of centralization and grouping
- Consolidated document flow, permitting accelerated quality controls
- Overall process monitoring by a neutral body

GLOBAL DISTRIBUTION SYSTEM

The global Distribution System (GDS) is the brain of the travel industry. It is a computerized network system which provides real-time information to companies such as airlines, hotels, car rental and travel agencies. Each of these sectors uses GDS to view the real-time inventory of services offered in the travel industry (e.g., number of hotel rooms available, number of flight seats available, or number of cars available).Travel agencies traditionally relied on GDS for services, products and raptor to provide travel-related services to the end consumers.

GDS is a reservation system utilised by service providers, its main customers are travel agents who make bookings through the suppliers' various reservation systems. GDS does not keep inventory; it is kept on the vendor's reservation system. The vendor's database will be linked in real-time through a GDS system. When a travel agency wants a reservation on a specific airline's service, for example, the GDS system sends the request to the appropriate airline's computer reservations system.

The best-known GDS systems globally are Amadeus, Sabre and Travelport (Galileo, Worldspan and Apollo).

ONLINE TRAVEL AGENCY – OTA

An online travel agency (OTA) is a web-based marketplace that allows consumers to research and book travel products and services, including hotels, flights, cars, tours, cruises, activities and more, directly with travel suppliers.

Every day, millions of travellers around the world use OATs to plan leisure and business travel. TO provide access to your potential guests in locations and at volumes that would be difficult for you to access through your marketing efforts. Additionally, OTAs provide market insights and tools for targeting travellers, securing and processing bookings, communicating with guests and managing reviews.

Advantages Of Online Travel Agents

- Low-cost method of selling accommodation services
- Reduced online marketing spend as OTAs invest in advertising to attract potential customers
- Impartial reviews give customers the confidence to book
- Users can easily compare various accommodation costs in one place

Disadvantages Of Online Travel Agents

- Commission rates are charged on every sale. It can range between 10-15% of the gross cost
- Restrictive cancellation terms
- Even if accommodation businesses use OTAs, the need for their website and booking engine does not go away
- Investment in a balanced multi-channel strategy may be needed to boost sales

How To Start An Online Travel Agency?

Travel agencies no longer inform customers about the availability of flights and rooms. They issue rooms and get a commission from the respective accommodation businesses. That is why most of the new travel businesses follow the OTA model.

Here Are Some Points You Have To Consider When Starting An Online Travel Agency.

- Register the name of your agency and if applicable, take a license as per your local laws
- Try to get a membership in IATA or any other reputed travel organization
- Gain more knowledge about the travel industry and particularly the nice you want to concentrate
- Get your travel website designed by a professional company like ColorWhistle
- Offer deals that focus on a specific geography. Focusing on a particular niche will also bring more success
- Publicize your business in the online space
- Utilize the power of blogging
- Create a good social media presence

THE BALLGAMES OF TOUR

"Great things are done when men and mountains meet."

– William Blake

TOUR OPERATOR

The package holiday business is intrinsically related to tour operators. The person or company that creates the package is known as the tour operator. The package holiday is then sold through a travel agency.

The term 'wholesaler' represents the tour operator in the distribution chain. This is because the tour operator is in charge of purchasing services in bulk and then distributing them to customers as a packaged product.

The Organisation for Economic and Cultural Development (OECD) define a tour operator as;

'Tour operators are businesses that combine two or more travel services (e.g., transport, accommodation, meals, entertainment, sightseeing) and sell them through travel agencies or directly to final consumers as a single product (called a package tour) for a global price. The components of a package tour might be pre-established or can result from an "a la carte" procedure, in which the visitor decides the combination of services he/she wishes to acquire.'

Today, tour operators have become highly competitive. They endeavour to achieve a high volume of turnover and maximum International and domestic market share by effectively operating. Moreover, the success of many developed and developing nations as tourist destinations depend heavily on a tour operator's ability to attract tourists, the development and promotion of tourism plants, the diversification of tourism products and their social responsibilities to develop remote and backward areas.

FUNCTIONS

1. Planning a Tour

The tour operator's most significant role is to plan a tour. Trip operators arrange a tour and create a tour itinerary that includes the origin, destination, and all points of interest in a traveller's journey. A potential tour operator can also advise incoming travellers on the many types of tour programmes available for their leisure or business travel.

2. Making Tour Package

Individual travel components are purchased individually from providers by tour operators and then combined into a package tour. Tour operators assemble numerous travel components into a finished product called a tour package, which is then sold to tourists at their pricing. Tour Operators are also responsible for creating tour packages.

3. Arranging a Tour

Tour operators provide tour packages and customise tours to meet the needs of tourists. To provide the finest experience to tourists/travellers, tour operators organise tour packages and numerous tourist activities.

4. Travel Information

Tour providers, regardless of their size, have provided travellers with essential travel information. This work is extremely challenging and complex. A tour operator must provide current, accurate, and timely information about destinations, modes of transportation, accommodations, sightseeing, immigration, health and security rules, and numerous permits required to travel in a specific place, among other things.

5. Reservation

It is a very important function of all types of tour operators and travel agencies. Tour operator makes all the reservation by making linkages with the accommodation sector, transport sector and other entertainment organizations to reserve rooms, and seats in cultural programmes and transportation.

6. Travel Management

Tour operators manage tours from the beginning to the end of the tour. A tour operator has the responsibility to look after the finer details of a vacation or tour such as hotel, accommodation, meals, conveyance etc. Tour operators provide travel guides, and escorting services and arrange all travel-related needs and want.

7. Sales and Marketing

Tour operators do sales and marketing of tourist products. Tour operators buy individual travel components, separately and combine them into a tour package, which is sold with their price tag to the public directly. Tour operators do the marketing of tourist destinations and tourism products to attract the attention of the tourists/travellers.

TYPES OF TOUR OPERATORS

Tour operators come in all shapes and sizes. Some are large, multinational organisations and others are small, independent businesses. Different types of tour operators develop products for different types of tourism. This can include the mass market, niche tourism market, special interest tourism, the luxury market, tailor-made products and dynamic packages.

Tour operators are categorized into four types. These are categories of the bias-based nature of the business and its operations.

1. **Inbound Tour Operators**
2. **Outbound Tour Operators**
3. **Domestic Tour Operators**
4. **Ground Operators**

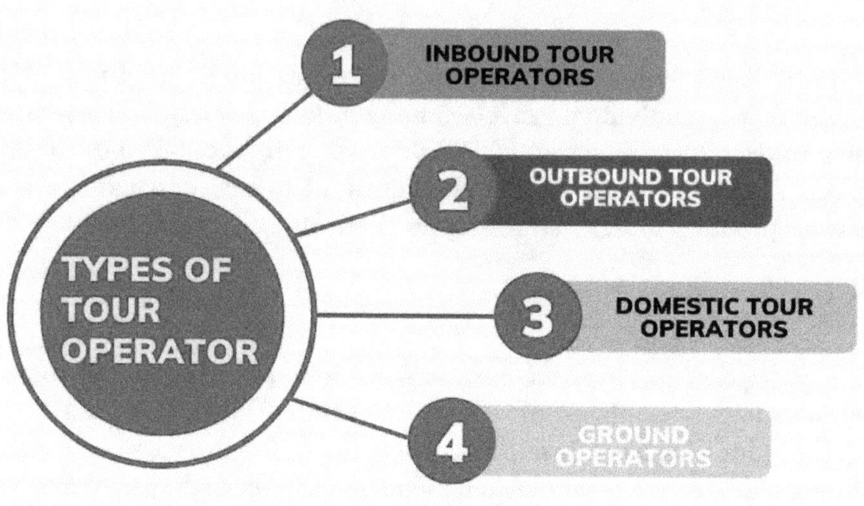

1. Inbound tour operators

An inbound tour operator facilitates inbound tourism. The aim of An inbound tour operator is aimsourists to a particular country or country. Inbound tour operators will often collaborate with local travel agencies and transport operators to facilitate travel arrangements for their customers.

For example, a group of American Tourists is coming through TCI Ltd. to India and the company makes arrangements and handles the group in India then TCI is called an inbound tour operator.

2. Outbound tour operators

An outbound tour operator facilitates outbound tourism. The aim of An outbound tour operator aimsurists out of a particular country or country.Outbound tour operators will often collaborate with foreign travel agencies and transport operators to facilitate travel arrangements for their customers.

For example, a group of American tourists going on a trip to India and Thomas Cook handle arrangements in America like ticket reservation, hotel booking etc. then Thomas Cook is called Outbound Tour operators in the context of America.

3. Domestic tour operators

A domestic tour operator facilitates domestic tourism. The aim of A domestic tour operator aims to travel within a particular country or country. Domestic tour operators will often collaborate with domestic travel agencies and transport operators to facilitate travel arrangements for their customers. Domestic tour operators will often also serve the inbound tourism market.

4. Ground tour operators

These are commonly known as handling agencies and their main function is to organize tour arrangements for incoming tourists on behalf of overseas operators. When a tour operator himself promotes beach holidays, wildlife holidays, adventure and heritage tours, and cultural tours at different places then the role of the ground operator becomes effective. It is the ground operator who by handling the incoming travellers at different places makes the tour successful.

TRAVEL AGENT V/S TOUR OPERATOR

There is a lot of confusion about the difference between tour operators and travel agents and what exactly makes them different. The main difference between a Travel agent and a Tour operator is the following:

- A travel agent is a person who has full knowledge of tourist products – destinations, modes of travel, climate, accommodation, and other areas of the service sector. He acts on the behalf of the product providers/principals and in return get a commission.
- Tour operator is an organization, firm, or company that buys individual travel components, separately from their suppliers and combines them into a package tour, which is sold with their price tag to the public directly or through middlemen.
- Tour operators are like wholesalers and travel agents are the retailers.
- A tour operator makes the package holidays up and the travel agents sell them on.
- Tour operator taking up the bulk of the responsibilities and his fee is much greater than a travel agent.
- A tour operator has the responsibility to look after the finer details of a vacation or tour such as hotel, accommodation, meals, conveyance, etc.

The wholesale travel agencies may offer or operate package tours or may specialize in developing tours for inbound as well as outbound travellers. They are often referred to as tour operators, but there is a difference between Wholesale Travel Agencies and Tour operators.

PRODUCTS AND SERVICES BY TOUR OPERATOR

Tour operators have several products and services that they sell, depending on their specific business model, business intentions and target market. A tour operator will typically package together two or more elements to form a packaged product, which is then sold at an inclusive price.

Examples include:

- Package holidays
- Accommodation
- Transfers
- Excursions
- Information on destinations
- Representative service in resorts

V
WRAPPING UP OF TOURS

"Do not follow where the path may lead. Go instead where there is no path and leave a trail"

– Ralph Waldo Emerson

PACKAGE TOUR

The term 'tour' was in vogue as early as 1670. The growth of packaging achieved something of a revolution in tourism. The idea of buying a package of travel, accommodation, and perhaps some ancillary services such as entertainment became established in Western Europe. This system succeeded in reducing the real price of travel abroad.

The tour package, means a pre-arrangement, prepaid trip that combines two or more travel components like airfare, airport transfer, accommodation, and other services. Practically, defining the tour package concept is a complex one rather understands.

The package tour business was planned and organized after the conduct of an organized package tour to Paris in 1855 by Thomas Cook. Package holidays can be escorted or unescorted given the needs and demands of customers. A package tour comprises a combination of two or more components of services to help the clients or customers save time & cost and avoid uncertainties.

Holloway defines a tour package as "a total tourism product consisting of transportation from the market area to the destination, accommodation at the destination and recreational activities promoted by the tourists."

TYPES

The tour operator is a consolidator or wholesaler in assembling primary and related services with a different price tag. However, packages are designed for independent groups. tours after making a comprehensive study and analysis. Broadly, all these package tours provide a bundle of services to the customers who are generally leisure and business tourists. The classification is made based on operation and types of services.

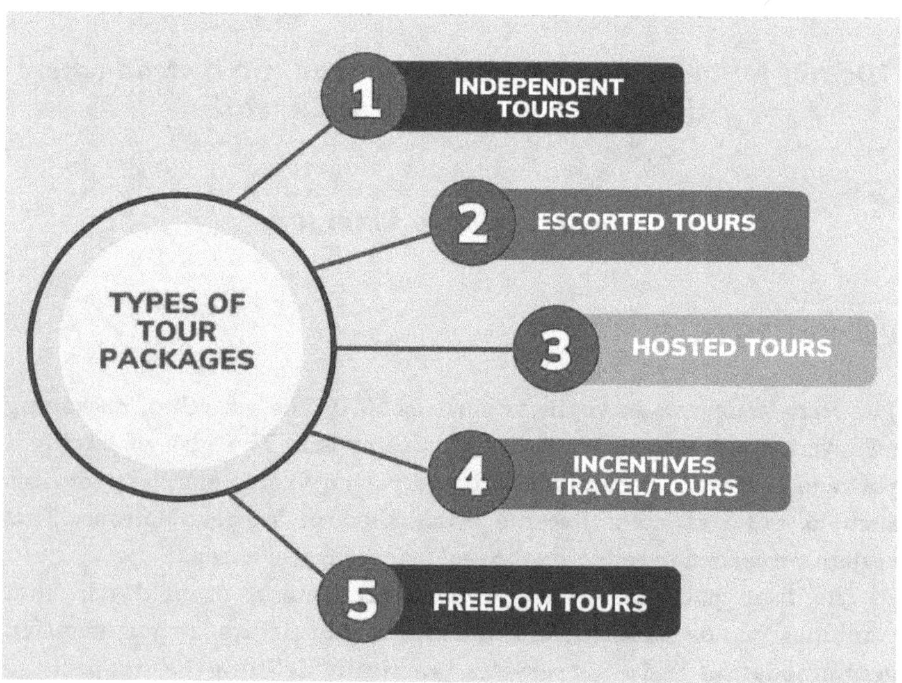

1. INDEPENDENT TOURS

A package tour is designed for independent tourists or free independent travellers. They are very much particular about selecting types of destinations, accommodation, and transportation as it suits the budget, comfort and time. Each element of service is purchased or a combination of components and services is included in the package. The independent tour largely includes domestic air tickets, hotel room services, processing of travel formalities, arrival and departure transfer and sightseeing. Other services include adventure sports, cultural events, and health-related activities that generally enhance the value of the independent tour. The cost of the package tour is relatively high as it includes most of the customized services. For example, high-end or budget travellers prefer independent tours.

2. Escorted Tour

An escorted tour is accompanied by qualified, trained, and experienced tour managers or guides, who provide information and assistance to the group at the origin, en route, and at the destination. about flight boarding, baggage handling, hotel check-in, meal arrangements along with interpretation about the places of tourist importance during sightseeing and all along the trip. The tour escort helps the group in check-in procedures, hotels, and food facilities and provides timely assistance and advice wherever and whenever required. Escort is expected to have the requisite knowledge, presence of mind and crisis management skills.

3. Hosted Tour

A hosted tour refers to a tour handled by another agency, ground operator or destination management agency as their representative of the tour operator, wholesaler or principal provider. They play the role of a host on behalf of a tour operator away for making ground services like cab, coach, guide, confirmation of hotel rooms, toll taxes, entry tickets, etc. as per the agreement. The wholesaler may not have its presence in a particular destination and thus takes the help of another agency to host the tour. A tour operator operating from outside the country may have a different host at different destinations in the host country. Hosting agencies take care of all the requirements of the tourists as per the contract.

4. Incentives for Travel/Tour

It is a motivational programme or a fully paid holiday which is given to the employees by the enterprises as a reward. Mostly in medium and large-scale companies and usually too-distant destinations to spur them in maintaining their track record, increase output, improve the image and earn the long period loyalty of the employees.

5. Freedom Tour

Working-class, these days, is inclined to travel but has limited disposable income. Such tours are designed as per the choices of the tourists. Tourists, individuals or groups of common interest, select services like travel mode, hotels, destinations, meal plans and activities etc. and plan for a tour. Such very flexible planning is assisted by tour operators and then they organise freedom trips. These are suitable for those people who want to decide where, when and how they want to travel and what they wish to do at destinations.

ELEMENTS

A package tour is a total of travel and other related services assembled to make it feasible and attractive to tourists. In designing package tours several elements play a vital role. What is to be included in a package tour largely depends and varies from one tour organization to another, from one country to another, or from one destination to another and from one market to another market. But there are certain well-defined travel services which always turn a part of a package tour irrespective of the tour operator/travel agency, destination and even the market condition. The elements of a package tour hold the success and sale of package tours in the travel market. Elements include;

1. Accommodation

Accommodation is a key component of a package tour and accounts for a significant portion of the entire cost. The category star hotels, resorts, business hotels, and international hotels are the primary service providers. Supplementary service providers include lodges, homestays, guest houses, bungalows, service flats, and so on.

2. Attractions/Sightseeing

One of the most crucial aspects of a package tour is including the most tempting sites. The best of experiences are determined by the type of sightseeing done, not to mention the inclusion of attractions in a package trip that must be scheduled in such a way that the best of experiences are obtained. From point to point, client happiness improves. The most thrilling activities should always be mentioned last, and the timetable should be designed accordingly. Sightseeing is, without a question, the backbone of the entire tour package because it provides the primary purpose of a tourist's visit to a location.

3. Transportation

Travelling is part of any tour. Transportation thus becomes yet another focal component of a package tour. The journey of a tourist from origin to destination involves tourtouristsement and it requires a suitable means of transport. Safe, comfortable and quick modes of transport are an inevitable component for tourists. Transportation modes can be air travel, railways, buses, ships, cars etc

4. Ground Services

Ground services are also an equally important element of package tours. Tourists cannot do away with ground services when they are at a destination. For local conveyance they need coaches, and cabs, to know about places they may need guides and interpreters to help them convey in the language of the land. Car rentals, luxury coaches, and other motor vehicle services are an active part of package tours enabling better travel with and around a destination.

5. Events and Activities

Events are of a different kind at destinations. Entertainment parks, theme parks, sports and leisure clubs are used for a variety of events and activities. Events such as meetings, incentive tours, conferences, conventions, exhibitions etc are sometimes part of certain package tours or package tours of such events are also offered by operators. Events and activities may be offered as complementary to tourists to add value to the package.

6. Insurance

Insurance companies have customised travel insurance for foreigner outbound travel for Indian travellers. Many nations have made it compulsory for visitors to have insurance before entering their countries. Insurance nowadays is included in the cost of the package or otherwise one can choose from travel insurance.

PLANNING AND DESIGN

The business of package tours is not free from risks like the season, rising prices and socio-political factors. The package tour is driven by quality services along with competitive prices. In this regard, there requires an extensive market survey to find the demand trends and tour operators accordingly formulate package tours to cater for the market. Thus, methodological tour planning is required to handle the risk factors and to improve the quality of a package tour.The tour operator assigns the responsibility of designing and formulating package tours to senior and experienced executives as the design of package tours makes the business andbreaks the business.

It is a multi-stage process that helps the tour manager develop and formulate a new package tour. First, the concept of designing a new package tour is taken a solid shape or form when collective ideas and experiences are consolidated. However, the field survey report is also assessed to understand the saleability and sustainability of package tours.

The following are suggested processes through which package tours may be designed.

- Initial research on destination and source market clarifies many drawbacks of a package tour and takes corrective measures for enhancing the quality and appeal of the tour.

- A well-structured itinerary is prepared with considerations of several do's and don't during the tour.
- Selecting the destination companies and authorizing them with the ground handling responsibilities.
- Vendors of primary and supplementary services are contacted and negotiated to obtain the best possible quotations.
- Costing of elements of package tours and pricing of package tours is done carefully.
- Selling the package tour directly or through retail travel can be done through a robust reservation system.
- Marketing and sales promotion helps in reaching the target market.
- Operation of the tour is carried out with the help of ground operators.

Besides these broad stages of developing, marketing and operating the package tours, other processes are implicitly associated with making the formulation and designing process complete.

SIGNIFICANCE OF TOUR PACKAGE

The Tour package is beneficial to travel companies, travellers, destinations and other organizations which are directly or indirectly involved in the tourism business. The main benefits are:

- Time Saver
- Increase the seasonality of a destination cost/price
- Earn foreign currency
- Better quality of products Professional services
- Wide variety of the tour package
- Provide bulk business to organizers

TOUR COSTING AND PRICING

Cost is the number of expenditures that may be actual or notional incurred on buying services. Tourism products are rarely identical, owing to factors such as geography, but also to the people and elements that make up the experience that a traveller receives. It can be extremely varied, and pricing methods might change as a tourism company's brand and market share grow. Even star ratings for hotels provide only a rough indication of what to expect in terms of pricing there are no established criteria. In the tour operating company.

Tour cost is represented as the total cost incurred or attributed to various elements of the package tour. In other words, we can say that the tour cost is the total of costs incurred to create or formulate a tour package.

In tour costing direct costs and fixed or variable costs are involved, Direct tour costs are those which are incurred and conveniently identified within a particular package tour. Fixed costs are those which are incurred even when one is selling or not selling any tour package.

ELEMENTS OF TOUR COST: -

- Accommodation Cost
- Transfer Costs
- Administrative Costs
- Research And Development Cost
- Travel Cost
- Marketing Cost
- Sightseeing and Activity cost
- Miscellaneous cost

PRICING PACKAGE TOUR

When quoting a price for a package tour, the tour operator takes great care. The price of a package is determined by the product's positioning and branding. Tour companies add their margins and package pricing after analysing trends. Furthermore, the tour operator has complete freedom to price the package, there are three sorts of typical pricing tactics.

1. Cost-Based Pricing

This type of pricing strategy is used to make over the cost to reach the breakeven point. It calculates the average cost of each element of services in the package tour and it adds a markup over and above the average cost to earn profit. This is a widely used technique.

2. Competition-Based Pricing

This pricing strategy takes a tab of the prices of its competitors to tag the price of its products may be set at the same price as a competitor or it may be a little above or below the price of the competitor.

3. Consumer-Based Pricing

This is a form of pricing that is primarily set to target customers by taking the affordability and the quantity of purchase into consideration. The inbound, domestic and outbound tour operators design the package tour taking the socioeconomic backgrounds of customers. All package tours are designed after assessing the market

Apart from the above-mentioned typical and age-old pricing strategies, the following are the pricing strategies used in the tour operation business.

Rack Rate Pricing

It is the full rate before discounts are given. It is generally printed in the tour brochures for the forthcoming season.

Seasonal Pricing

A wide mix of pricing for package tours is set to cater to low, high and shoulder seasons as tourism is largely driven by the season.

Last Minute Pricing

it's the common practice of giving discounts from the daily quoted price to close a booking. In group travel, tour operators offer some additional services or discounts on the prices to get a minimum booking to operate the tour.

Per Person Pricing

This type of pricing is set per person or for each category of service. It can be per adult or child or additional person.

Per Unit Pricing

It is a set of prices for one unit of package. It may include husband and wife with children (cost-free). Sometimes, the package includes room, transfer and sightseeing costs. The room rate generally includes breakfast as per the European Plan (EP).

FACTORS AFFECTING THE TOUR COST

- Seasonality
- Foreign Exchange fluctuations
- Competitors'rs price strategy
- Increase in other costs.
- Impact of liberalization and globalization
- Promotional pricing/ special discounts

VI
THE STORY OF TRAVEL PLANS AND HANDOUTS

"If you reject the food, ignore the customs, fear the religion and avoid the people, you might better stay home."

– James Michener

ITINERARY

A travel itinerary is a list of activities connected to a trip that includes destinations to be visited at specific times as well as modes of transportation to get between them.An itinerary is a key and significant component of a tour package.It is designed to identify the origin, destination and all the enroute stopping points along with the transportation, accommodation and other services on a travellers trip an itinerary has various portions and these portions are known as segments.

Since a travel itinerary might serve different purposes for different kinds of travellers, a travel agent must know all the characteristics of her/his target customers. A typical business traveller's itinerary might include information about meetings, events and contacts with some time for leisure travel, efficiently.

The quality of a tour package is determined by the suitability, nature and comprehensiveness of a tour itinerary. It is generally printed in tour brochures but only after the clearance from the expert team as it includes logical inclusion and sequential arrangement of a variety of features.

TYPES

Classification to remind individual responsibilities:

1. Tourists' itinerary

Tourists" itinerary is given to a particular tourist for his reference as part of the package tour. A tourist expects the tour to be organized as per the itinerary mentioned in the package tour,

he/she has purchased. For planners, it is important to check its feasibility.A tourist itinerary is a reference for the tourist to follow during his journey like points of halt, hotel, time taken between two points, meal plans, activities, attractions to visit etc. apart from arrival and departure points/time and check-in check-out time. Tour operators are expected to strictly follow the itinerary. If they intend to change or modify it, that should be only in the interest of the safety and security of the guests. And they should consider their client before doing that.

2. Tour manager's itinerary

The Tour manager's itinerary includes the complete details of the whole tour from day one to the last day. Apart from the general details listed in a tourist itinerary a tour manager's itinerary also carries information about alternative arrangements, contact details, quick references, differential rates and tariff details, and details of coach drivers and escorts and guides. This helps him/her to have complete control over the smooth conduct of the tour as well as to execute contingency plans if required at times.

3. Escort or guide's itinerary

An escort or guide should know exactly where the group is going, what activities and events are planned, how the trip will be timed, and other pertinent information. An escort or guide's vast experience, awareness of actual ground obstacles, presence of mind, and readiness to face a crisis all contribute to a tour's success. Because the escorts are physically present with the group/tourist throughout the travel, they are required to deliver and maintain the company's image.

4. Vendor's itinerary

Vendors play a critical role in ensuring that the client's itinerary is followed. As a result, it is unavoidable to be informed of the precise sections of the itinerary to make the appropriate arrangements ahead of time and give the visvisitorsmplete satisfaction when they arrive at their destination. For example, a hotel might throw a surprise welcome event for a group based on the type of the group and the time of arrival, or it might offer specific services to boost service satisfaction and value.

5. Coach driver's itinerary

The itinerary of a typical coach driver contains group arrival points and times, pick-up points and times, turnaround locations, prohibited driving regions, tourist activities, other entertainment activities, parking spaces, entry points, and drop-in points, all of which have particular times. For example, a driver may be ordered to drive slowly where it is specified in his itinerary so that tourists can get a better view of a monument and take photographs. A copy of the client's itinerary looks like a bus driver's schedule, but with the additional information described above. This aids the driver's coordination with the escort and group management.

THINGS TO REMEMBER

The following information should be kept in mind when planning an itinerary:
- Always have an interesting and attractive heading for the itinerary
- Show the date and time clearly
- Draw special attention to highlights of the trip.
- Always break the itinerary up into paragraphs with new dates

· Provide as much information about the attractions and activities included in the tour plan, as possible
  · Always use the 24-hour clock,
  · Allow sufficient time for each highlight
  · Place each highlight in a logical order, remember to give priority to saving client travelling time and cost
    · Try to finish each day with a special highlight, if possible
    · Distance must be realistic, try to use the 100km per hour rule
    · Never make fake promises (that is, you will have a fantastic sea bath if, the entry to the sea is restricted.)

CONTENTS

- Write clearly and to the point.
- The client must want to travel immediately to their preferred destination when they read your itinerary.
- It must however leave the client wanting to travel to discover the destination for them.
- Give them just enough information to whet their appetite.
- Never use the word etc in an itinerary
- If your itinerary is for five days or more, you can include one day at leisure but be sure to suggest a variety of things to do on that day, that would match the client's profile.
-

STEPS IN DEVELOPING/PLANNING A TOUR

Step 1 – Research other tours in the marketplace

Careful planning is required when developing an itinerary for your tour. A helpful exercise is to take a tour which will be similar to the tour you wish to develop and obtain copies of other tour brochures for comparison. This will help you develop ideas for your tour, give you an idea of what is already in the market, give you detailed information on terms and conditions and provide possible ideas for brochure design and its content.

Step 2 – Name your tour: ....

Step 3 – Map out the duration, frequency and departure point of your tour

When will your tour depart? .... am/pm
    When will your tour return? .... am/pm
    How often will your tour operate? .... per/ wk
    Where will the central departure point be? ....
    Will you offer accommodation pick up? Yes No

Step 4 – List the major locations and highlights of your tour

Where will your tour travel to?

Step 5 – Research your tour content and commentary

List the main topics you wish to include in your commentary, such as flora, fauna, history, and culture, as well as the main points to consider with each of these topics and the resources you will use to find the information.

Step 6 – List any third-party activities, attractions, entrance fees and Inclusions.

Step 7 – Obtain permission to access private and public properties.

Step 8 - Perfecting your tour timing

It is crucially important to map out your tour itinerary accurately to ensure that you arrive on time for activity and meal stops and return to your original destination at a reasonable time.

Step 9 – Test driving your tour itinerary

It is very important to do several 'try runs' of your tour itinerary to ensure you get the timing right. It is also a good idea to invite people who have some knowledge of the industry and are prepared to give you constructive comments, to do a tour.

ITINERARY SAMPLE

Tour Itinerary Pilgrimage and Leh Tour
    Duration: 8 Nights / 9 Days
    Destinations Covered: Delhi - Lucknow - Sravasti - Lumbini - KushinagarVaishali - Patna - Nalanda - Rajgir - Bodhgaya - Varanasi – Delhi
    Day 01: Arrival Delhi on arrival at Delhi International Airport, you will be met and transferred to your hotel. Check into the Hotel and relax. Overnight stay will be in Delhi.
    Day 02: Delhi - Lucknow - Sravasti After breakfast, in time transfer to the airport to board a morning flight for Lucknow. Arrive Lucknow and check into your hotel. Afternoon, enjoy an excursion toSravasti, a place where Lord Buddha spent his last 20 rainy seasons. Visit the ancient villages of Maheth and Saheth, which have the remains of the Jetavana Monastery. These Sravasti villages also have the ruins and relics of Jain temples. The overnight stay will be at Sravasti.
    Day 03: Sravasti - Lumbini After breakfast, we drive to Lumbini, the birthplace of the Lord Buddha, in Nepal. Arrive at Lumbini and check into the Hotel. Afternoon, enjoy a visit to the location where Lord Buddha is believed to be born. The overnight stay will be at Lumbini.
    Day 04: Lumbini - Kushinagar After breakfast, we drive to Kushinagar, where Lord Buddha breathed his last. Arrive at Kushinagar and check into your hotel. After freshening up, visit the Mahaparinirvana Temple and Ramabhar Stupa. The overnight stay will be at Kushinagar.
    Day 05: Kushinagar - Vaishali - Patna After breakfast at the hotel, we proceed to Patna by surface, en route to visit Vaishali. Vaishali is one of the important ancient historic cities of India, where Lord Buddha preached his last sermon. Arrive at Patna and check into the Hotel. The overnight stay will be at Patna.
    Day 06: Patna - Nalanda - Rajgir - Bodhgaya After breakfast at the hotel, we drive to Bodhgaya visiting Nalanda and Rajgir along, en route. While

Rajgir was an ancient capital city, Nalanda is a famous Buddhist site known for its ancient university. Arrive at Bodhgaya and check into the hotel and relax. The overnight stay will be at Bodhgaya.

Day 07: Bodhgaya After breakfast at the hotel, visit the sacred Mahabodhi Temple - where the Buddha attained enlightenment under a Bodhi Tree after years of search for the truth and knowledge. Afternoon, enjoy a sightseeing tour of Bodhgaya visiting Niranjana River, Sujata Village and many beautiful monasteries. Evening, visit the Mahabodhi Temple for prayer. The overnight stay will be in Bodhgaya.

Day 08: Bodhgaya - Varanasi After breakfast at the hotel, we drive to Varanasi. Arrive and check into the Hotel. Evening free at leisure. The overnight stay will be at Varanasi.

Day 09: Varanasi - Delhi Early morning visit to the lively Ghats of the Ganges to enjoy the breath-taking view of the sunrise and rituals performed by thousands on its banks. Enjoy an unforgettable boat cruise on the Ganges, indeed a wonderful experience. After lunch, we proceed to Delhi by road. After dinner, in time transfer to the international airport to board the flight for your onward destination or way back home with sweet memories of India.

BROUCHERS

A brochure is a folded informational or advertising paper document that can be folded into a template, booklet, or leaflet. The main purpose of working out a brochure is to present the information about the tourism product and services while persuading the customer to buy this product. Thus, an effective travel brochure should attract the customer and include a message which can stimulate the customer's positive buying behaviour.

Tour Brochure is a small booklet or pamphlet, often containing promotional material or product information about destinations or travel services. A brochure (also referred to as a pamphlet) is a type of leaflet. Brochures are most commonly found at places that tourists frequently visit, such as museums, major shops, and tourist information centres. Another type of brochure is interpersonal brochures, which are brochures based on other people. The two most common brochure styles are single sheet and booklet (folded leaflets) forms.

According to Bhatia, "since tourism is an intangible product which cannot be pretested by the prospective consumer before the purchase, the brochure becomes the important channel of informing a customer about the product and also motivating him to buy the product". Potential customers react to the information in brochures as effective advertisements. That is why a brochure should be well designed and organised.

The most common types of single-sheet brochures are the bi-fold (a single sheet printed on both sides and folded into halves) and the tri-fold (the same, but folded into thirds). A bi-fold brochure results in four panels (two panels on each side), while a tri-fold results in six panels (three panels on each side).

Brochures need to be visually appealing and convey the right amount of information, and brochures should be comparable to other brochures in the industry. When drafting a copy of a brochure, one should make sure not to include any unacceptable (illegal) clauses or misleading information.

CONTENTS

- Name of the Travel Company
- Means of transport
- Details about destinations
- Itinerary
- Accommodation, types, location, meals
- Name of the overseas representative
- Duration of each tour
- Booking, reservation and cancellation conditions
- Details of other services – insurance, currency, entertainment travel documents required
- Details of price

TIPS FOR DESIGNING BROCHURES

- White space is GOOD! Avoid the folded lines!
- Get a professional print job.
- Use simple, easy-to-read fonts.

- Make your text conversational and use bullet points and minimal text - be concise!
- Be consistent with your design.
- High-quality, exciting images and use 'hero' images, don't overcrowd with photos.
- Make your headings and subheadings clear and bold. z Maps can be very useful, but be sure to make them clear.
- Clearly explain the product or service, and what all is included.
- The top third of a brochure is the most important - make it count!
- Determine your unique selling features and highlight them.
- Include all details - prices, times, location, validity dates, booking etc.
- y display contact details for bookings (phone/fax, email and web addresses)
- Leave room on the back of the brochure for a travel agent's stamp.

QUALITIES OF A GOOD BROCHURE

1. A Good Cover

This is the first thing that people will see and it should immediately answer three questions: 1. Who is advertising? (Name of the business) 2. Where it is located? 3. What they are selling? Make the cover visually compelling and keep it simple. Use professional quality images.

2. Description of the Benefit

Comprehend to potential customers not only what is offered, but why they will enjoy it. This will require knowledge of the target audience, so adequate research is required to complete this stage. Create a personal message to that audience letting them know why they specifically should participate in given offerings.

3. Call to Action

The brochure should focus on one specific objective. If you are announcing new offerings, make sure the brochure explains them and their benefits. A brochure that is intended to describe a travel product should be detailed and provide plenty of pictures and descriptions. You should include a statement telling people what you want them to do next and how they can become involved.

4. Product Explanation

Describe the facilities completely and include attractive photographs. Include information about special services, promotions and events. Tell them what differentiates you from the competition.

5. Recreational Activities

List not only the facilities and activities available to your guests but also any public sites that they may be able to take advantage of during their stay. Entertainment is an important part of travel, so be sure you include all the fun things your guests will experience with your travel product.

6. Geographic Information

List the address, contact details and a map to help people find you. If you are located in a place that is difficult to get to, include comprehensive directions. Include your website address if you have one.

7. Pictures

Travel is a very visual product category. People want to see where they are going and only high-quality professional images can achieve this. Include several photos that best showcase your product. Be careful, however, not to mislead people by using old photos or pictures that misrepresent your offerings.

VII
PEDDLING THE TOUR

"The beautiful thing about learning is that no one can take it away from you."

-B.B. King

TOURISM MARKETING

Marketing is the action or business of promoting and selling products or services, including market research and advertising. According to Kotler, " Marketing is a social and managerial process by which consumers obtain what they need and want through creating and exchanging product services and values with others." He has emphasized more on wants, needs, satisfaction, demand, and marketers.

Travel and tourism marketing is the systematic and coordinated implementation of business policies by both private and public sector tourism organisations operating at the local, regional, national, and international levels to meet the needs of identifiable tourist groups while generating a reasonable return.

At the World Tourism Organisation seminar, held in Ottawa in 1975, on Testing Effectiveness of Promotional Campaigns in International Travel Marketing, marketing was defined as "a management philosophy which, in light of tourist demand, makes it possible through research, forecasting, and selection to place tourism products on the market most in line with the organisation's purpose for the greatest benefit". Three aspects are suggested in this definition:

1) Marketing is a thought process related to a situation which matches and balances the needs of the tourists with the needs of the destination or the needs of the organisation's designing and providing tourism-related services.

2) Tourism research is an inherent part of tourism marketing which culminates in the identification and selection of target markets based on market segmentation.

3) To have proper placement of tourism products and services, the marketing concepts of positioning and product life cycle are of great significance.

IMPORTANCE OF TOURISM MARKETING

The tourism industry provides a combination of different products and activities, which ranges from small taxi operators to the largest airline or hotel chains. The concept of change and survival is as important to the tour operators as they have to deal with various vendors in the tourism market. It would, therefore, become imperative to understand what is tour marketing planning, especially for the long-term survival of an ant tour/ company.

A tour marketing plan is a structured guide for carrying out marketing operations. It provides a common structure and focuses on all the company's management activities.

- It provides a clear direction for marketing operations.
- It coordinates the resources of the organization to eliminate confusion and misunderstanding and achieve cooperation.
- Identifying different market segments.
- Setting targets/goals.
- Identifying the organization's strengths and weaknesses.
- Corporate mission and goals.
- External and Internal Audit.
- Business situation analysis.
- Creating the objectives.
- Providing an effective marketing mix strategy.

- Monitoring the plan.

Thus, it has become imperative to discuss the tour marketing segment, tourist generating market, and tour marketing mix before developing a tour marketing plan.

FEATURES OF TOURISM MARKETING

The success of any segment of the travel and tourism industry depends on how well the products and services are marketed. Tourism being a service industry, marketing of services is different from most products because what is being sold is an experience rather than a tangible product. Tourism marketing is concerned about understanding the needs of its potential customers (tourists) and satisfying those needs by offering a suitable product. In this section, we will briefly discuss some features of tourism products.

1. Inseparability

Services are consumed and experienced by a customer simultaneously and as such makes it impossible to demonstrate the product being offered before it is consumed. For example, a tourist who is travelling from Delhi to Mumbai will consume the services offered by the airline and at the same time feel the experience.

2. Perishability

This is another important aspect of tourism products. Tourism products are intangible and cannot be stored like other tangible products. For example, if a bus having a capacity of 50 seats leaves with 30 filled seats only, the vacant seats cannot be stored and therefore become useless or so to say they perish.

3. Ownership

In tourism products, a customer buys only the experience. The transfer of ownership does not take place. For example, in the case of tourism products like hotels, houseboats and aeroplanes, the customer experiences only the stay in a hotel or a houseboat but does not own the product.

4. Heterogeneity

The other aspect of tourism products is their heterogeneity. Tourism products are a combination of several services provided by people. The high involvement of humans results in variation in behaviour from one consumer to another. For example, an employee at a bank counter, may not behave in the same manner as every customer.

MARKETING MIX

The term "marketing mix" is a foundation model for businesses, historically centred around product, price, place, and promotion. The marketing mix has been defined as the "set of marketing tools that the firm uses to pursue its marketing objectives in the target market". In services marketing, typically comprises 7 Ps that are, product, price, promotion, place, packaging, positioning and people, made up of the original 4 Ps extended by process, people and physical evidence.

1. PRODUCT

The first P of the marketing mix is the produce product role of the marketing mix in tourism is to make the tourists aware of what the company is trying to market or promote. The product for tourism may be a bus tour, a hotel stay or a cruise. The product or service is especially targeted to the tourist market but can range from a tangible product, such as a souvenir to an intangible product, such as a bus tour of the city.

2. PRICE

Pricing is another major aspect of the role of the marketing mix in tourism. Pricing has to be set so that any competitors that are offering the same business or substitute business are comparable. In other words, if the tourist activity is kite sailing and there are two other kite sailing companies in the area, the company that is opening a new kite sailing company needs to see what their competition is charging.

3. PLACE

The place is the role of the marketing mix on how the product or the service is connected with the client, customer or tourist. If it is a tourist product, then this portion of the marketing mix entails distributing the product to store retailer shelves or other ways of getting it to paying tourists. When it is a tourism service, it typically entails drawing the tourists to where the service is.

4. PROMOTION

Promotion is the role of the marketing mix in tourism. It encompasses all of the ways that the company markets and advertises the business. This may include typical types of marketing, such as placing ads in tourist magazines and offering discount coupons in travel guides. It may also include going from hotel to hotel in the area and leaving a postcard or flier for the service at each hotel room door.

5. PROCESS

The tourist would look at the quality aspect of service apart from the processing time. Quick service with quality is always preferred by a customer. If a tourism firm fails to satisfy this, a customer would switch over to the competitor who serves the tourist better. Thus, an efficient process, which would reduce the customer time without deteriorating the quality, should be adopted by a tourism organisation to retain the tourists.

6. PHYSICAL EVIDENCE

The common element in all services including tourism services is that they are tangible, physical, and controllable aspects of any service sector. Physical evidence can be used to build a strong association in the mind of tourists and also to differentiate the service from that of competitors. This element relates to the external and internal appearance of any tourism-related organisation. For example, the customer in a restaurant would look for hygienic food in addition to its external and internal appearance of it.

7. PEOPLE

As the people are involved in offering services to customers, their performance plays a vital role in the tourism sector. The behaviour and attitude of the service personnel in a hotel, transport or travel agency play a key role while performing the services which are visible to the tourists. They play an important role in attaining customer satisfaction.

MARKET SEGMENTATION

In marketing, market segmentation is the process of dividing a broad consumer or business market, normally consisting of existing and potential customers, into sub-groups of consumers, known as segments based on some type of shared characteristics. In dividing or segmenting markets, researchers typically look for common characteristics such as shared needs, common interests, similar lifestyles, or even similar demographic profiles.

According to Middleton, "Market segmentation is the process whereby producers organize their knowledge of customer groups and select for particular attention those whose needs and wants they are best able to meet their product."

Tourism segmentation involves a division of the prospective market into identifiable groups. The reasoning behind this is that a tour package can be sold more effectively if efforts are concentrated on those groups which are the most potential.

- Segment the tourists' generating markets.
- Identify the network of intermediaries.
- Identify the nature of demand for one's product.
- Identify the prospective tourists.

An effective market strategy will determine exactly what the target market will be in an attempt to reach only those markets. The target market is that segment of a total potential market to which the tourist attraction would be most saleable.

The tourism market segmentation can be broadly divided into the following types –

i. Geographic

Geographic market segmentation is done by considering the factors such as tourists' place of origin. This factor is important as the tourists belonging to different places are brought up with different cultures and show different traits and behaviour. It is the most basic type of segmentation.

ii. Demographic

This segmentation is done by considering the tourist's gender, age, marital status, ethnicity, occupation, religion, income, education, and family members.

iii. Psychographic

The marketing people do this segmentation by taking into account the psyche of the tourists. They gather information about the tourists' interests, attitudes, way of living life, opinions, and overall personality.

iv. Behavioral Segmentation

In this segmentation, prospective tourists are segmented based on their knowledge, attitude, use or response to the tour product. Under this segmentation, the marketing strategies of a four-company include:

- **User Status**
- **Usage Rate**
- **Loyalty Status**
- **Buyer Readiness Stages**
- **Attitude**

v. Price Segmentation

Price ranges often come in handy in segmenting the tourist markets, such as

- Those who want to take a low-priced vacation.
- Those who may take a moderately priced vacation.

Price ranges communicate to the tourists the quality expectation of a product along with the producer's image. While determining the price of a tour package a tour planner must understand the paying capacity of the tourist.

TARGET MARKETING

A target market is a group of customers within a business's serviceable available market at which a business aims its marketing efforts and resources. A target market is a subset of the total market for a product or service.

The target market typically consists of consumers who exhibit similar characteristics (such as age, location, income or lifestyle) and are considered most likely to buy a business's market offerings or are likely to be the most profitable segments for the business.

DEFINING TARGET MARKET

-

Segment The Market

Segment your business's serviceable market according to its demographics, geographics, psychographics, and behavioural patterns.

Identify Your USP

Your unique selling proposition is what differentiates you from your competitors. It is why the customers will prefer your product over others.

Analyse Your Customer Base

If you're already in business, the best way to define your target market is to collect your customer data and analyse it.

Analyse Your Competitors' Customer Base

Analyse your competitors' customer base: Who do they target through their marketing efforts? Where do they sell their products?. You can either select a similar target market or choose a slightly different segment.

VIII
HAWKS IN TOURISM

"Once a year, go someplace you've never been before."

~ Dalai Lama

TOURIST BUYING BEHAVIOUR

Buying Behaviour is the decision processes and acts of people involved in buying and using products. Consumer behaviour is one of the most researched areas in tourism. This studies why a tourist chooses a particular destination and what are the driving factors that influence his decision to travel.

FACTORS AFFECTING TOURIST BEHAVIOR

The following factors immensely alter tourist behaviour –

- *Geographical Factors*

Some physical factors like geographical and climatic conditions, facilities and amenities available at the destination, and advertising and marketing conducted by tourism businesses alter the decision-making of the tourists.

Social Factors

A few social factors such as a person's social network, provide first-hand information that can alter a person's decision of visiting or not to visit a particular place.

Place of Origin

There can be a broad spectrum of tourist behaviour depending upon the place they belong to. North Americans like to follow their cultural framework. Japanese and Korean tourists like to visit places in groups.

Tourism Destination

It is a major contributing factor to altering tourist behaviour. If a destination has all basic provisions such as electricity, water, clean surroundings, proper accessibility, and amenities, and has its significance, it largely attracts tourists.

Education of Tourist

The more educated the tourist is the wider range of choices, curiosity, and knowledge of places he would have. This drives the decision-making when it comes to choosing a destination.

PLOG'S MODEL OF TOURIST BEHAVIOR

Plog classifies tourists into three categories as described below –

i. Allocentric (The Wanderers)

A tourist who seeks new experiences and adventure in a wide range of activities. This person is outgoing and self-confident in behaviour. An allocentric person prefers to fly and explore new and unusual areas before others do so. Allocentric enjoy meeting people from foreign or different cultures. They prefer good hotels and food, but not necessarily modern or chain-type hotels. For a tour package, an allocentric would like to have the basics such as transportation and hotels, but not be committed to a structured itinerary. They would rather have the freedom to explore an area, make their arrangements and choose a variety of activities and tourist attractions.

ii. Psychocentric (The Repeater)

A tourist falling in this category is usually non-adventuresome. They prefer to return to familiar travel destinations where they can relax and know what types of food and activity to expect. Such tourists prefer to drive to destinations, stay in typical accommodations, and eat at family-type restaurants.

iii. Midcentric (Combination)

This category of tourists covers the ones who swing between the above said two types.

HENLEY CENTRE MODEL OF HOLIDAYMAKING

A British Consultancy of Futurology, Henley Center has divided the tourists into four phases –

Phase I- Bubble Travelers

They do not have much money as well as knowledge. They prefer packaged tours. They long to observe different cultures without being a part of them. They travel mostly out of curiosity.

Phase II- Idealized Experience Seekers

They are confident tourists with the experience of foreign tours. They are flexible and comfortable. They prefer tour offers made for individuals.

Phase III- Seasoned Travelers

These tourists are more affluent than the idealized-experience seekers. They are more confident to experiment and experience different places and environments. They are more adventurous and prefer individualistic tours.

Phase IV- Complete Immerses

These tourists have an intention of immersing completely in the foreign culture, heritage, culinary experience, and language. Their holidaying is well-planned but not well-structured. In the above phases, the tourist goes through different phases and therefore also seeks different tourism options or destinations.

IMAGE BRANDING AND POSITIONING

In marketing, brand management begins with an analysis of how a brand is currently perceived in the market, proceeds to plan how the brand should be perceived if it is to achieve its objectives and continues with ensuring that the brand is perceived as planned and secures its objectives.

Brand positioning is "the act of designing the company's offering and image to occupy a distinctive place in the mind of the target market" in the words of Kotler. In other words, brand positioning describes how a brand sits in customers' minds according to the company.

A brand image on the other hand according to Kotler "is the set of beliefs, ideas, and impression that a person holds regarding an object". Therefore, brand image is the general impression of a product held by current and/or potential consumers.

As a marketing tactic, branding personifies the tourism business. It gives a voice, looks, personality, and values. Ultimately, a well-defined brand helps to appeal to the right audience, as well as leave a lasting impression. Travel agencies develop a distribution channel mix that makes up an effective portfolio for determining the patterns of marketing activities, target markets, tangibility, and trust created for travel shoppers. Brand awareness and brand image influence the strategies of distribution channel management. With the rapid growth of Internet-based distribution channels, the relationship among these channels is becoming more complicated, and to maximize revenue wholesaler travel agencies may adopt different marketing distribution channels for different types of guests.

It is proved that individuals having prior knowledge associated with a particular product category, can remember some features of the product approximately twice more than those who don't have prior knowledge of the product category. Also, by associations linking to a brand, connection points cause a specified image of the brand to be developed.

DISTRIBUTION SYSTEM IN TOUR OPERATION BUSINESS.

Distribution channels and consumer purchasing behaviour varies from market to market so it's important to understand the structure of the distribution system specific to each target market. The travel distribution system is a complex, global network of independent businesses. This network includes a series of distributors or intermediaries, who play a specific role in the development, promotion and purchasing process of tourism experiences.

Travel distributors allow broadening the customer base far beyond the reach of the marketing budget. They are important to the inbound tourism industry as overseas consumers still heavily rely on the advice of local travel experts when planning and booking their trips, particularly in long-haul and emerging markets. Travel distributors can also provide market intelligence, insights and advice on a specific market. The travel distribution system covers all the channels through which an international traveller can buy the products.

IX

TOUR ADMINISTRATION

"We travel, initially, to lose ourselves; and we travel next, to find ourselves."

~ Pico Iyer

TOUR MANAGEMENT

Tourism Management involves the management of a multitude of activities such as studying tour destinations, planning the tour, making travel arrangements and providing accommodation. It also involves marketing efforts to attract tourists to travel to particular destinations.

RESERVATION SYSTEM

An up-to-date reservation system should be developed and implemented to put a package tour programme into operation. Depending upon the nature and size of the business, a suitable system may be adopted. There are two systems in operation:

1 Manual system
2 Computerised reservation system.

1.

MANUAL SYSTEM

The reservation department should be situated within the operator's chat room. The full programme of flights and hotels is pasted on the walls of this room, so as availability can be quickly scanned by the telephone staff. The chart will draw attention to any changes in the programme. The Reservation department should ensure that changes are brought to the attention of agents and customers.

○

Procedure

The sale of tours is done through the travel agents. Deal with the inquiries and booking telephone made by these agents as well as the public. Travel agents require quick connections to tour operators at the reservation system. Once a travel agent is connected to the reservation department the agent identifies himself and his company. The operator checks on the availability of the tour in which his client is interested. If the tour is available, it will be reserved either under the option or as a definite booking. An option is usually held by the operator until the end of the following day when they will be automatically released unless the agent has phoned to convert to a definite booking. In both cases, the reservation department provides the agent with a code number to identify the booking. Once a booking is definite, the client completes the tour operator's booking form and this is sent together with the appropriate deposit by the agent to the operator, the booking code being shown on the form. The tour operator booking forms are usually required to arrive in the tour operator's office within a week or again the booking will be automatically released

○

Hotels and Flights

Actual control of flights and hotel sales can be handled in a variety of different ways. A usual method is to use coloured tabs hanging on pegs adjacent to each flight and hotel. As bookings are made a tab is removed from each and inserted into a booking shown on the exteriors of the envelope such as:

- Date of booking
- 'Lead' name of customer
- Number of seats reserved
- Agent's identification
- Sales office reference.

Once, all the coloured tabs are removed from a peg, it will signify that the flight on a hotel is fully booked. Whenever any cancellation is found, return the tab to the pegs.

RESERVATION BY MAIL

On receipt of the Booking Form in the mail, it is immediately processed by the reservation section. The reservation staff makes the booking as 'definite in the records and arranges for a confirmation to be sent to the agent. The booking forms are passed on to the account section. An invoice is raised by the account section which along with confirmation marked to the agent. Now, it is the agent's responsibility to ensure that his client remits the final payment due by the date given in the invoice. Upon receipt of the final payment, the tour operator can issue the tickets, along with the itinerary and vouchers and despatch them to the agents.

2.

CENTRALISED RESERVATION SYSTEM (CRS)

The tourism product is an amalgamation of many fragmented products It must be made easy for customers to buy, taking full account of the flexibility of packaging, pricing and value-added. components. The tour operators need to have rapid access through the channel of distribution to the ultimate consumer to gain maximum exposure for their products.

A computer reservation system or a central reservation system (CRS) is a web-based software used by travel agencies and travel management companies to retrieve and conduct transactions related to air travel, hotels, car rental, or other activities. It was originally designed to be used by airlines but was later extended to be used by travel agencies and Global Distribution Systems (GDS) to book and sell tickets for multiple airlines.

The main objective of CRS was to make a one-stop service shop and eliminate physical and geographical distances between mediators and consumers. With universal coverage, these distribution systems provide information for airlines, hotels, car rental companies, travel agencies, corporations and more.

To facilitate a smooth and dynamic flow of information, the first CRS was introduced as an experiment in the 1960s by airlines to keep track of sold seats. In 1963, SABRE (Semi-Automated Business Research Environment), the world's first CRS was introduced by American Airlines. After that, CRS became the primary means of distributing air travel information and had a major impact on competition within the airline sector. In 1976, travel agencies started using them and henceforth became a universal feature of the tourism industry.

GLOBAL DISTRIBUTION SYSTEM

A global distribution system (GDS) is a computerised network system that is owned or run by a company and facilitates transactions between service providers in the travel sector, primarily airlines, hotels, car rental agencies, and tour operators. The GDS mostly employs real-time inventory from the service providers (such as the number of available hotel rooms, seats on flights, or automobiles). In the past, travel agents relied on GDS for services, goods, and prices to offer final customers travel-related services. Travel agencies, both online and in-person, are the main GDS clients. They make reservations using a variety of vendor-operated reservation systems.

The GDS system keeps a copy of the passenger name record (PNR) that is kept in the airline reservations system. A passenger's full itinerary will be stored in the passenger name record in the GDS system if they book an itinerary through a travel agency. Each airline they fly with will only have access to the portions of the itinerary that pertain to them. The best-known GDS systems globally are Amadeus, Sabre and Travelport (Galileo, Worldspan and Apollo).

TOUR PLANNING: NEW DESTINATION

For the introduction of a new destination on the tour schedule, proper tour planning is necessary. The strategy ought to be developed well in advance. Two years are typically allowed before the first departure is anticipated. The launch date and backward working should be explicitly stated in the plan. About nine to ten months before the last leaves, the final price must be decided. A tour operation program's overall time frame can be broken into the following:

First Phase

Research and Planning Phase

- Study the economic factors influencing the future development of package tours.
- Identification of likely selection of destinations
- Make an in-depth comparison of the capacity of each destination.
- Decide on the capacity of each tour, duration and departure dates

Second Phase

Negotiations Phase

- Initial negotiations with printer including dates for printing vouchers.
- Negotiation with airlines for charter flights.
- Negotiation with hotels, transfer services, optional excursion operators Artwork and text under development at design studies, with layout suggestions.
- Establish hotel prices and arrange for contact with hotels and airlines.
- Contact transfer services.

Third Phase

Administrative Phase

- Determine exchange rates.
- Estimate selling price based on inflation.
- Proofs from printers.
- Recruitment and training of reservation staff.
- Final tour pricing to printer
- Establishment of brochures printed.
- Reservation system

Fourth Phase

Marketing Phase

- Brochures on market destination among agents.
- Initial agency sales promotion including launch.
- First public media advertising and trade publicity through press etc.

Fifth Phase

Departure Phase

- Peak advertising and promotion to trade and public
- Recruitment and training of resort representatives etc.
- Final Tour Operation

TOUR PREPARATIONS

PRE TOUR-PREPARATIONS

1. Find out what tours have been assigned to him or her or the Tour Assignment.

2. Research the tour if it is unfamiliar.

3. Checks to see if any special holidays occur during the tour.

4. Attends a briefing meeting and asks about anything unclear.

5. Reviews the material given. (Especially, passengers' names and any special client information or requests.

6. Be aware of the composition of the group (children, teens, seniors, if foreign what is their nationality, their language culture etc.)

7. Review the itinerary

8. Be aware of the vouchers or tickets that will be needed

9. Know your vehicle to be used, the plate number and the name of the driver and/or the coordinator.

ON-TOUR PREPARATIONS

1. Be Punctual

2. Make sure you have the complete name of the guests, the cash advances and tour vouchers.

3. Check your transport amenities (microphones, trash bins, etc)

4. Meet and greet your group by introducing yourself to customers/guests/tourists.

5. Check Luggage (if any)

6. Hand out essential documents

7. Review /discuss the general itinerary for the tour as well as the rules and regulations. Announce the inclusions or exclusions of the tour and what to expect.

8. Establish commentary with and among the group.

9. Deliver your spiel and/or commentary.

10. End your day by announcing the next day's itinerary/ program and give proper instructions

11. End your day or tour by thanking your guests/ tourists.

POST-TOUR PREPRATIONS

1. Report to the company, handling required forms and describing any unusually events that occur.

2. Prepare and submit the Tour guide's report immediately after the trip.

3. Accomplish the financial report with the necessary receipts, vouchers and other documents.

4. Liquidate if necessary.

5. Company sends follow-up notes to clients thanking them for the business.

TOUR BOOKING

Technique Of Tour Booking

The technique of booking a tour requires the following information

- Booking source
- Tour identification
- Departure date
- Departure place (city)
- Passenger identification
- Client preferences

The Booking Source

The booking source is identified by the following:

- **Name of the travel agency**
- **Address of travel agency**
- **Telephone number of the travel agency**
- **The ARC and IATA numbers.**
- **TOUR IDENTIFICATION**

A tour is identified by the tour code or name.

DEPARTURE DATE AND CITY

These are required to determine availability and book air and hotel space. Departure from inland cities requires air transportation to and from the gateway point.

PASSENGER IDENTIFICATION

Passengers are identified by

- **Name**
- **Address**
- **Telephone Number**
- **Form of payment**
- **The number of travellers in the party**
- **The number of adults per room**
- **The age of children etc.**

Client's Preferences

- **Client's special preferences are required, such as:**
- **Smoking or non-smoking accommodation**
- **Dietary restrictions**
- **Need for facilities for disabled travellers**
- **Option activities**
- **Side tours etc.**

X

THE BOSS IN TOUR'S

Travelling is not something you're good at. It's something you do, like breathing."

~ Gayle Foreman

TOUR MANAGERS

The tour manager is often called upon to offer a sight-seeing commentary on the country or region through which he is travelling and acts as a source of information. These are employed by tour companies or tour operators to supervise groups of tourists participating in the tour. Depending upon the size of the tour company and the number of types of groups, he is handling, he may be called 'tour escorts', 'tour leaders' or 'tour manager'. He is employed mainly based on his experience.

As a representative of the industry, the tour manager holds the position of tourist. His job requires a broad liberal arts background and demands such skills as writing, researching and public speaking. He must know about finance and accounting and must understand the complexities of the tourism business.

Qualification

A tour manager should be professional in the full sense of the word. He must acquire the necessary educational background and training to carry out his duties.

Education and Training

Until recently the only training in the field of travel, transportation, and tourism was acquired on the job. Now, several schools, colleges, universities and institutes offer training courses. The industry is pleased with growing professionalism. The tour manager should have a broad background in the social sciences, particularly history, geography, political science, languages, and cultural appreciation. He must have training in methods of dealing with the varied situations that can and will arise while on tour.

PERSONALITY

Education and training mean nothing unless you can communicate this expertise to your clients. The essence of a tour manager's job is communication. To be an effective communicator, he should possess the following traits:
1. Leadership
2. Tact
3. Patience and understanding
4. Sense of humour.

APPEARANCE

Proper dress is essential, as is good grooming. Your wardrobe should reflect the type of tour you are managing.

ETHICS

A tour manager has certain definite ethical responsibilities to:

1. The company that employs him
2. The providers of services to the tour
3. The clients on the tour.

He must be guided by a strong code of ethics and common sense.

ROLE AND RESPONSIBILITIES OF A TOUR MANAGER

Tour managers ensure travel arrangements run as smoothly as possible and provide holidaymakers with practical support throughout their trip. In-depth knowledge of a particular area or region is essential and you may act as a tour guide during the tour. Tour managers are also sometimes known as tour directors.

- Accompany groups travelling by coach, or in some cases by car, boat, train or plane
- Welcome groups of holidaymakers at their starting point and announce details of travel arrangements and stop-over points
- Check tickets and other relevant documents, seat allocations and any special requirements
- Help with passport and immigration issues
- Assist holidaymakers with check-in and settle them into their accommodation
- Communicate a range of information on itineraries, destinations and culture
- Inform passengers of arrival and departure times at each destination on the itinerary and ensure that all members of the group are back on the couch before departing from each stop
- Develop a specialist area of knowledge
- Use professional knowledge to answer questions from holidaymakers and to fulfil their expectations of the tour

- Make sure all travel arrangements run according to plan and that accommodation, meals and service are satisfactory
- Organise entry to attractions and transport, such as car hire
- Ensure that the tour is running smoothly for individual members of the group
- Respond to questions and offer help with any problems that arise, ranging from simple matters, such as directing a member of the group to the nearest chemist, to more serious issues, such as tracing lost baggage
- Deal with emergencies, such as helping a holidaymaker who is ill or those needing to contact family members urgently
- Make contact in advance with places to stay or visit to check details and arrangements
- Liaise with hotels, coach companies, restaurants and other clients
- Advise about facilities, such as sights, restaurants and shops, at each destination
- Occasionally make accommodation bookings on proposed dates
- Organise and attend tourism events, conferences, workshops, seminars and exhibitions
- Write reports and maintain records
- Provide feedback after a tour as part of a debrief session.

TOUR MANAGER BRIEFING

The major part of tourist's satisfaction is not only the tour, itinerary management, on-time arrival at tourists' places, visiting right places, having the opportunity to visit shops, having refreshments, but, also interaction with the tour guide. The main objective of tour briefing is that the tour is delivered properly to the client or tourists.

Tour briefing helps the guide to tailor information to the needs of the group. He should be briefed about: -

- Group size: how many people are travelling in the group.
- Language: What is the common language of the people in the group?
- Age: How old the group members are? What is their average age?
- Place: What else the itinerary includes?
- Area: Special interest of the group.

- VIP: Is there any VIP in the group? Special instructions about the VIP.
- Special requests: What are special requests made by the client?
- If he has to collect vouchers or other payments as people join the tour.
- Meeting place: When and where to meet with the tourist's vehicle?
- Duration: Total number of days and nights of the tour.
- Cities to be visited with the map.
- Services to be provided in each city.
- Whether meals are included or not included.
- Restaurant addresses location, telephone, contact number and person.
- Hotel with address and phone number.
- Agents address with his contact details like telephone number etc.
- flight details like flight number, arrival, departure, terminal, airport
- Exchange rates
- Airport taxes
- Meeting points at the airport (departure)

TOUR DEPARTURE AND ARRIVAL PROCEDURES AT THE AIRPORT

People take guided tours because they want a peace of mind trip, clear of worries, troubles and the need to make decisions. So, it's the job of a travel company to help the tourists in all respect.

Tour companies provide detailed information about the documentation to prospective tourists. The experience will acquaint them with what is required by the clients and the destination they are visiting. Check the documents of all the members at the time of their initial registration before the departure of the tour. Verify the validity of all travel documents and give them back to the members following an inspection. These documents are very important and so must be responsible for their loss. Some of these documents are:

1. Passport and its validity
2. Record all tour member's passport numbers on a rooming list
3. Visa and its requirements
4. Tourist cards
5. International Health Certificate with the seal of the Head of the Department and their verification.

If a tour member's documents are not in order or incomplete, assist him/her in obtaining the proper papers at the next destination. The cost involved such as taxi fare, visa fees etc. are to be borne by the member.

DEPARTURE PROCEDURES

- While departing from the airport one has to report at the counter to hand over the ticket and get the boarding pass.
- Luggage is also deposited at the same counter.
- The Handbag may be carried on the flight. Its quantity, weight; size depends on the travelling class. Different airline companies have different policies.
- Passengers have to keep their passport, and identity cards ready.
- After reaching the airport, passengers may convert currency from money changers. Various banks and reputed companies have money changers at the airport. As this is the last point to changing local currency into an international one, the tourists must be careful to acquire some of the minimum required international currency.
- After collecting the boarding pass traveller has to report at the immigration counter. The immigration counter checks the documents and all belongings of passengers. They put a stamp on the passport. In case stamping is missed out, the passenger may contact FRRO, otherwise, he will face a problem at the arrival point.
- Tour guide must have a thorough knowledge of these prerequisites and he should inform the group about the formalities well in advance.

ARRIVAL PROCEDURES

- After arriving at the airport passenger has to report at the immigration counter and submit a form (disembarkation form). The disembarkation form is for people coming from a foreign country. Some information about his source of the journey, cash carried by him is collected here.

- After getting through the immigration, he collects his luggage from conveyor belts.
- After collecting baggage passengers may convert currency from money changers. Various banks and reputed companies have money changers at the airport.
- Air journey is very systematic. Even first-time travellers can travel without any hassle. Signs are used everywhere. If requested, airline companies have the policy to help first-time travellers.
- To receive tourists from the access point You must have seen many people waiting outside the airport terminal with the name of a visitor on the hardboard known as a placard. When the tour guide is working for the company, he has the placard of the company.
- A Person travelling with the tour group i.e. Tour Escort meets the tour guide appointed by the travel agency. Initially, the tour guide helps them to get the luggage and properly arrange it in the coach. He asks them about their travelling experience.

HANDLING EMERGENCIES

Be prepared for emergencies Keep calm, use your common sense and think before you act Make a quicdecisionson when the unforessituationstion suddenly arises. Some of these emergencies could be

1. Sickness of member/s
2. Death of member/s
3. Worker's strike
4. Bankruptcies of a business
5. Natural disasters lead to closed highways, means of transport, and other facilities.

-

Illness of a Client

Health is a vital factor in touring. Be prepared to deal with any health problem that may arise Members must get medical care when needed. When a client complains of illness encourage him to visit the doctor or nurse and make an appointment for him. Hotels have the facility to have house doctors on call. You should never diagnose a client's ailment and give anyone any medicine. Let the doctor make the diagnosis. In remote areas where doctors are not available, ask the hotel manager to see if there is a doctor in the house. There may be a doctor among the guests or tour members. If the hotel cannot help, try the police. The telephone directory will supply the necessary information. A client who is too ill to travel on the tour for a few days may wish to re-join the group later. If possible, to make such an arrangement, inform your company of the change.

Death of a Member

If a member of the group dies firstly, notify the local police. If the death occurs in a country other than the deceased's home country, advise the appropriate consulate or embassy. If these offices are closed, send an urgent telegram to the consul or ambassador, giving all of the facts at your disposal. Secondly, advise the tour company of the situation.

Remain with the body until the police have completed their reports and if necessary, until the consulate has assumed. responsibility for the body. Inform the company of the names of the police and consulate officials who have taken the charge.

XI
TOUR PILOTS

. *"I travel because it makes me realize how much I haven't seen, how much I'm not going to see, and how much I still need to see."*

– Carew Papritz

TOUR GUIDES

According to the World Federation of Tourist Guide Association (WFTGA), "Tourist Guide is a person who guides visitors in the language of their choice and interprets the cultural and natural heritage of an area which person normally possesses an area-specific qualification usually issued and/or recognised by the appropriate authority".

A tourist guide is a person who has a thorough knowledge of the destination or site as she/he is knowledgeable about the particular destination and its attractions. Along with the insight of a destination in terms of culture, food, flora and fauna, traditions, festivals etc; the tourist guide will add his/ her own theme/ style to make it a memorable trip for the guests.

HISTORY OF GUIDING

One of the oldest occupations/professions in the west is tour guiding. Pond (1993) divided the development of tour guides and the history of guiding into four eras:

FIRST PHASE (3000 B.C. TO A.D.500)

There are several references in history from the Roman Empire to the Middle Age, throughout the renaissance and into the Modern Age. During the time of the great empires, tourism underwent its first significant development. Travelling at this time was dangerous, uncertain, and time-consuming. The ancient Persians, Assyrians and Egyptians used to travel through the surface (land) and the waterways.

Guides are named "periegetai" (leaders around) or exegete (explainer) in the Greek language. The tasks of "Proxemos" were to help fellow people travel abroad. The first travel writer, Herodotus was able to provide numerous references to guides.

SECOND PHASE (A. D.500 TO A. D.1500)

The second phase spans around a thousand years, from 500 A.D. to 1500 A.D., during the Middle Age, a time between the fall of Rome and the beginning of the Renaissance. The most common kind of journey taken by middle- and upper-class people was a religious pilgrimage.

The period between Rome's fall and the Renaissance is known as the Dark Ages (500 A.D. and 1508 A.D.). Rome's fall has led to a decline in trade and the economy in general and a decline in travel desire. Guides' positions are pathfinders, protectors, security escorts and even bridges during this era are stressed to ensure safe passage. A guide was paid a large fee, according to Casson, a historian, because he not only led the way but also created safe behaviour for the travellers.

THIRD PHASE (A.D.1500 TO AROUND 1700)

The third phase covered the period of the Renaissance and the Grand Tour, approximately A.D.1500 to around 1700. Young people from affluent families, commonly known as "Grand Tourists," went on excursions during the Renaissance for cultural and educational purposes.

These individuals (tourists) were supposed to broaden their knowledge by travelling great distances while being escorted by a guide who informed them of the tourist destinations to be seen. During this time, guides acquired the nickname "cicerone." The word cicerone derives from Cicero, the most esteemed tour guide in European society. The guide was expected to be well versed in many practical subjects, and areas, be articulate and be multi-lingual.

Fourth Stage (MODERN AGE)

During the 18th and 19th, centuries travellers to and within the New World were explorers rather than pleasure travellers. The first travellers were ordinary often indigent explorers who travelled a lot to find a new way of life. No evidence exists of organized training for guides before the 12th century other than the company training given by the Thomas Cook Travel Agency. England was one of the 1st countries to regulate and train guides.

The competitive, aggressive approach by tour guides toward visitors and watching others prompted the London Country Council and the Regent Street Polytechnic to open a training course for guides in 193. European guides have been widely regarded as having the most advanced training and the highest guiding standards in the world.

Israel guides are the world's best trained, most highly respected and best-paid guides. After the 2nd World War, the London Country Council re-established its guide training program at Regent Street Polytechnic in 1949 and the "Approved Guides" which accredited guides with a badge and certificate. Guiding training and regulation in most European countries served as a model for the world where, until recently, few advancements in professional status have been achieved.

TYPES OF GUIDE

There is a generic definition of "tour guide" which was established in the section above. Tourist guides are certified and licensed; and assist the guests/ visitors in seeing the place in an excellent, unique way. Tourists Guides can be classified based on four different criteria. Let us study the many kinds of tourist guides available:

CLASSIFICATION BASED ON LICENSING AUTHORITY

As you are aware, the major difference between a Tourist Guide and Tour Escort is that a Tourist Guide is a licensed Professional while Tour Escort may or may not be licensed. In India, we find three licensing authorities for Tourist guides and we can classify guides based on the licensing authority. They are:

1. SITE/ LOCAL CITY GUIDES

Guides are selected and trained by local bodies and given licenses to operate as local guides. For Example, the Archaeological Survey of India (AST) has introduced a new guide policy that will be implemented in all of its monuments across the country. According to this new policy, ASI will select individuals based on their merit and grant them a guide licence, and they will then need to undergo a six-week training. The programme is provided by ASI. These licensed guides will be able to operate only in the monuments of ASI.

2. STATE-LEVELVEL GUIDES

The State Tourism Development Corporation of all the states of India, conduct a process of selection of Tourist guides who are then trained and given license to operate as Tourist Guide only within the border of that one state. For Example, Odisha Tourism Development Corporation will give the license for operations only within Odisha.

3. REGIONAL LEVEL GUIDES

Ministry of Tourism (MoT), Government of India selects Regional Level Tourist Guides who can operate beyond one state. According to MoT, the five jurisdictions or areas of operation of the Regional Level Guides would be as under:

i. **NORTHERN REGION:** States of Delhi, Haryana, Himachal Pradesh, Jammu & Kashmir, Punjab, Rajasthan, Uttarakhand, Uttar Pradesh, and Union Territory of Chandigarh.

ii. **SOUTHERN REGION:** States of Tamil Nadu, Andhra Pradesh, Karnataka, Kerala and Union Territories of Pondicherry & Lakshadweep

iii. **WESTERN & CENTRAL REGIONS:** States of Maharashtra, Madhya Pradesh, Chhattisgarh, Gujarat, Goa and Union Territories of Dadra & Nagar Haveli, Daman & Diu.

iv. **EASTERN REGION:** States of West Bengal, Bihar, Jharkhand, Orissa, Union Territory of Andaman & Nicobar Islands.

v. **NORTH-EASTERN REGION:** States of Arunachal Pradesh, Assam. Meghalaya, Manipur, Mizoram, Nagaland, Sikkim & Tripura.

CLASSIFICATION BASED ON EMPLOYMENT TERMS

Tourist Guides can be classified based on the employment contract that they have or the way they pick up guiding jobs. They can be:

1. FREELANCE GUIDE

Guides are not attached to any particular tour and travel company or hotel or any other organisation. They are freelancers and can work with any tour company or provide their services to the tourist on site. They can also be in a contract with fea w companies and pick and choose assignments as per their choice.

2. STAFF/TOUR COMPANY GUIDE

Tourist Guides are on the payroll of only one Tour company and are salaried Tourist Guides

3. VOLUNTEER GUIDE

Volunteer Guides, also known as a docent. They are the guide who are working free of charge or volunteering on a siteThe document specifically works at a museum. An example will be the Volunteer guides at National Museum, New Delhi

CLASSIFICATION BASED ON TIME COMMITMENT

Tourist Guides can also be classified based on the time that they give to the vocation.

1. FULL-TIMELINE GUIDES

Tourist Guides who work as Tourist Guides all through the year are full-time Tourist Guides.

2. SEASONAL GUIDES

The season for inbound tourists in India is from October to March. There is some Tourist guide workbook only with foreign inbound tourists during the inbound season as tourist guides and not during other months of the year.

CLASSIFICATION BASED ON PLACE OF GUIDING (SPECIALISATION)

1.

Heritage/Cultural

A cultural or heritage guide is someone employed on a paid or voluntary basis who conducts paying or non-paying tourists around an area or site of historical, cultural and heritage importance utilizing guiding and interpretation principles.

2.

Nature Guides

Nature tour guides lead groups to natural attractions, national parks, and other outdoor locations where wildlife and scenic locations are the focus of the tour. These guides are experts in the natural sciences and can engage visitors with their knowledge of biology, geology, and the history of the location.

3.

Eco-Tourism

The Guides who communicate and interpret the significance of the environment, promote minimal impact practices, enensurehe sustainability of the natural and cultural environment, and motmotivateurists to consider their own lives about larger ecological or cultural concerns are known as Eco-Tour Guides

4.

Museum

A Museum Guide is someone who accompanies visitors on a visit to a museum, providing them with information about the various objects in the museum's collection; and also responsible for making sure that the visitors do not violate the museum regulations.

5.

On-site-

A guide who takes tourists on a tour of a particular site only and is available only at that particular site is known as an on-site guide. OAnsite guide conducts the tour of a specific building or a limited area.

6.

City Guides

A tourist can take a tour of the city by motor coach, van, taxi or hop-on, hop-off bus, or as part of a walking tour and the guide who points out and comments on the highlights of the city is called a city guide.

7.

Specialised Guides

The specialised guide has particular skill sets that are highly unique to match the demands of a tourist. These guides may condbikesbike physically demanding and unusual. At times they are also known as Adventure Tour guides, depending upon the specialization.

8.

Step-on Guides

This kind of guide is more commonly seen in the United States of America and is usually free-lancguidedes. They are considered specialists who meet a touring group, 'steps on the coach or van to give informed overviews of the area being toured; and the steps as the tour continues to other areas.

9.

Personal/Private Guide

Personal or private guides are also a type of city guide and at times they are driver and guide at the same time. These guides have their vehicles and since the area to cover is small, being a driver cum guide is economical. For example - an island-tour

10.

Cruise ship Tour Guides

Guides that work for cruise ships can be classified as cruise ship tour guides or shore excursion guides. These guides take groups of tourists for the shore excursion and are employed permanently with the Cruise Ship Operators.

ETHICS IN TOUR GUIDING

Ethics in professional life is very important, and that's what differentiates a successful guide from an unsuccessful Guide. It is the responsibility of the Tourist Guide to follow these work ethics. The Ethics in tour guiding applies primarily to three areas of the job:

1. Content of tour guiding

Whenever information is being provided to the tourists,

- A Guide should be truthful and honest about the information
- Never make makeup motion
- Provide all the products and services that were advertised and promised in the tour itinerary

2. Behaviour during and after guiding

A guide needs to behave in a manner that reflects his work ethic A guide should ;

- Deliver tour guide services in a way which is sensitive to local social, economic and environmental issues
- Meeting the principles of Responsible Tourism
- Never ask tourists to go on tours without going through your employer or asking for tips.
- Do not buy or sell (illegal) items or make a profit from tourists
- Always be loyal to the tour company that employs you for the tour
- Declare your income for tax purposes
- Not pay bribes or charge tourists for special services outside of the itinerary.

3. Management of tours and activities

Professional ethics are reflected in the way a tour is planned, organised and managed.

- The guide should not change the itinerary or places/ shops for special commissions if it changes the quality and value of the tour.
- Avoid missing out on any activity and stops at sites.

Role of a Tourist Guide

A tour guide is someone the group of tourists follow from site to site. The primary role of a tour guide is to be -

- ### *Leader*

  The guide must be a leader who can move a group of tourists and someone the tourists will gladly follow from site to site.

- ### *Educator*

  Being knowledgeable about the region, locality and site is very important. The information imparted should be correct and shared in a manner that does not offend anyone, either the guests or the hosts

- ### *Host*

  The guide is the host for the tourists and should behave accordingly. The guide should not forget to share information about local tradition and culture and behave with the politeness of a host.

- ### *Interpreter*

As an interpreter, the ide should interpret local traditions and culture for the tourists. He must also be the interpreter between the host community and the guests since they might have a language barrier.

Public relations

The guide is the public face of not only the tour company but also of the country or destination a tourist group is visiting.

QUALITIES OF A TOUR GUIDE

1.

Punctual

Punctuality shows that one respects the other person enough to respect their time. Tourists, especially international tourists are very careful about time and as a tour guide, one should be the first to arrive at every meeting.

2.

Good communication skills

Having good verbal communication, good presentation, public speaking as well as having multiple language skills constitutes good communication skills of a guide.

3.

Pleasing personality

Self Confident, Friendly, Eloquent/Articulate personality will be perfect for a guide as she/he needs to hold the attention of tourists, and group members.

4.

Polite and Respectful

It is important that guide is aware of cultural differences between a tourist and his/her own country of origin and be respectful. Further, people with disability must be handled with respect and politeness, and also compassion but never pity or apathy.

5.

Enthusiastic and friendly

The guide must be enthusiastic about the tour programme and be proactive while interacting with the tourists. This will ensure that the tourists participate in the tour and have a great experience.

6.

Tactful and patient

The guide needs to be patient and tactful as at times tourists can ask some questions that might go against the value system of the guide but the guide must be flexible and prepared to tackle unpleasant situations.

7.

Open to questions and assertive

Guides must be accommodating and open-minded enough for the tourists to ask questions. At the same time, they should be assertive enough to avoid and lead the group away from unpleasant questions and situations.

8.

Honest and trustworthy

The guide must be honest and trustworthy enough for the guests to feel comfortable with him/her and accept the knowledge shared.

9.

Resourcefulness with good memory

The guide must be resourceful enough to collect unusual information about the tourist destinations and sites to make the trip unique. Being able to retain historical facts (fond of History) as well as cultural aspects of the destinations is very important. JIVE

10.

Sense of humour

sense of humour can build many bridges and make us many friends among strangers. An Outgoing personality with a good sense of humour is very important for guides who meet strangers regularly as a part of her/ job.

11.

Good Health

Tour guiding generally means man-hours of standing as well as walks daily. It is therefore important that a guide must bear good health and physical fitness to meet the demands of the job

12.

Time Management

Every experienced guide knows that they have their fixed times on a tour and that they must maintain a constant eye on the clock and readjust their mental plan continuingly. This relationship and constant readjustment between time, distances, and guest experience is an integral part of guiding and must become second nature to a guide's thinking.

Unexpected delays or opportunities often arise, and with every delay or addition of a stop or activity, the time/distance/experience matrix must be readjusted.

TOUR INTERPRETATION

The term interpretation is defined by many scholars in different contexts but among the most promising one in the context of culture as defined by the task force of Canada "Interpretation is a communication process, designed to disclose meanings and relations of our cultural and natural heritage, through involvement with articles, artefacts, sceneries and sites."

It should be said that interpretative communication is not mere presenting information but a particular communication strategy that is used to interpret the specific language to an understandable language of the visitor. Interpretation is an informative activity which aims to disclose meanings and relations through the use of unique objects through first-hand experience and descriptive media, rather than simply to communicate accurate information.

ROLE OF INTERPRETATION

- To increase the visitor's understanding, awareness and the appreciation of nature of heritage of site resources;
- To communicate information relating to nature and culture, including natural and historical processes, ecological relationships and human roles in nature;
- To include people in nature and history through first-hand (personal) experience with the ordinary and cultural environment;
- To affect the behaviour and attitudes of the public concerning the right use of natural resources, the preservation of cultural and normal heritage, and the respect and concern for the normal and cultural environment;
- To provide an enjoyable and meaningful experience; and
- To increase public understanding and support for the agency's role, its management objectives and its policies.

Overseas Representative

A resort representative needs to be employed to carry a large number of packages to a particular destination. This representative could be a native of the host country or the generating country. Employment of local persons as the representative has certain advantages. These people are better acquainted with local customs and geography, fluent in the language of the country and have good Local contacts, especially with the police, shop-keepers, customs or language of their client.

The overseas representative's role at the resort is more demanding. During the busy tourist season, they have to work seven days a week for 24 hours a day to cope with emergencies. Usually, he is given a desk in the hotel's lobby. He pays visits to different hotels where guests are residing. His main duties include:

1. Handling of guest inquiries
2. Advising on currency exchange
3. Advising on shopping
4. Organising and supervising social activities at the hotel
5. Publishing and booking optional excursions
6. Handling special requirements of customers
7. Handling of complaints
8. Acting as an intermediary for clients
9. Interceding with the hotel's proprietor, police or other local authorities.
10. Handling other miscellaneous problems such as:

- Lost luggage
- health;
- Occasional deaths,
- Relocation of customers whose accommodation is inadequate or where overbooking occurs, and
- Re-booking of flights for their customers whose plane changes as a result of emergencies.

DUTIES OF OVERSEAS REPRESENTATIVES

The overseas representative is very busy on the days of arrival and departure of groups. His main duties on arrival and departure of groups include:

- To accompany groups returning house on the couch and to the airport,
- To ensure that departure formalities at the hotel have been compiled with, 3. To arrange to pay any airport or departure tax due
- To greet incoming clients and accompanies them to the hotel on the transfer coaches,
- To ensure that check procedures operate smoothly, going over rooming lists with the hotel manager before he bills the tour operator,
- To arrange and organise welcome parties on behalf of the tour operator for the clients on the first night of their holiday,
- In addition, these representatives are expected to spend some time at their resort bases before the start of the season. This will help them to know the site and report back to companies on the stand of tourist facilities. He pinpoints any discrepancies between the brochure descriptions and reality.